Mistake Proofing for Lean Healthcare

Lean Tools for Healthcare Series

Series Editor: Thomas L. Jackson

PUBLISHED

5S for Healthcare

Standard Work for Lean Healthcare

Kaizen Workshops for Lean Healthcare

Mapping Clinical Value Streams

Mistake Proofing for Lean Healthcare

FORTHCOMING

Just-in-Time for Healthcare

Continuous Flow for Healthcare

Quick Setup for Healthcare

Kanban for Healthcare

Mistake Proofing for Lean Healthcare

Rona Consulting Group & Productivity Press

Samuel Carlson, MD, FACP and Maura May, Editors

CRC Press
Taylor & Francis Group
Boca Raton   London   New York

CRC Press is an imprint of the
Taylor & Francis Group, an **informa** business

A PRODUCTIVITY PRESS BOOK

CRC Press
Taylor & Francis Group
6000 Broken Sound Parkway NW, Suite 300
Boca Raton, FL 33487-2742

Library of Congress Cataloging-in-Publication Data

Mistake proofing for lean healthcare / Samuel Carlson and Maura May, editors.
    p. ; cm. -- (Lean tools for healthcare series)
    Includes bibliographical references and index.
    Summary: "Mistake-proofing is an improvement technology that uses a device or procedure, also called a poka-yoke, to prevent defects or errors during a process. Mistake-proofing in healthcare can improve the quality of patient care and services; correct conditions in the process that allow for errors or mistakes; support ideas from knowledgeable staff to improve a process or area; and reduce costs to the organization by eliminating duplication of work. This user-friendly book introduces the concepts of Zero Quality Control (ZQC) and Poka-Yoke Systems. Using healthcare examples, this practical text explains the concept of mistake-proofing through the use of margin assists, key terms, and how-to-steps"--Provided by publisher.
    ISBN 978-1-4398-3743-6 (paperback : alk. paper)
    I. Carlson, Samuel (Physician), editor. II. May, Maura, editor. III. Series: Lean tools for healthcare series.
    [DNLM: 1. Quality Assurance, Health Care--methods. 2. Efficiency, Organizational. 3. Health Facility Administration. 4. Total Quality Management. W 84.41]

RA971
362.1068--dc23
    2015005188

Visit the Taylor & Francis Web site at
http://www.taylorandfrancis.com

and the CRC Press Web site at
http://www.crcpress.com

Contents

Preface

The book you are holding is intended to give you powerful knowledge that you can use to make your healthcare workplace safer and more productive, and your job easier and more satisfying. It's about a way to provide defect-free healthcare services and products by catching and fixing mistakes and errors *before they can cause defects.*

Mistake proofing is one of the secrets of lean value streams and the just-in-time production of services. Elimination of defects means no need for extra, or "buffer," resources to do rework or to replace defective supplies or products. It means work can flow smoothly, without the disruption of uncaught errors. It means safer, more reliable, and more effective healthcare for patients, customers, and staff.

The mistake-proofing approach you will learn about here is based on a system called Zero Quality Control (ZQC for short) developed by Shigeo Shingo, a Japanese industrial engineer known for his skill in improving production processes. Zero Quality Control does not mean *no* quality control. On the contrary, it means quality control (QC) that ensures not just fewer defects, but *zero defects* (Z). The ZQC system, now commonly called "mistake proofing," is being applied in many industries and types of work, including healthcare.

Mistake-proofing systems focus on correcting *the conditions in which processes are performed*—not on blaming people for making mistakes. Shingo recognized that it is human nature to make mistakes or forget things. Punishing people for unintentional mistakes doesn't eliminate defects. In fact, it makes it harder to expose the sources of errors so that they can be corrected.

Shingo's solution is explained in *Mistake Proofing for Lean Healthcare*. This book has been adapted from *Mistake-Proofing for Operators: The ZQC System*, which was in turn developed from Shigeo Shingo's book, *Zero Quality Control: Source Inspection and the Poka-Yoke System.*

Mistake Proofing for Lean Healthcare provides an overview of the five key principles of lean healthcare management (Chapter 2). It then introduces the main concepts and benefits of mistake proofing. It discusses common reasons that errors and defects occur and explains how to catch errors before they become defects.

You will learn about the idea of ensuring quality *before* the process instead of afterward. You will also see examples of different types of "poka-yoke" or mistake-proofing devices and methods that can automatically provide quick feedback and action. Poka-yoke systems work to immediately inform someone that there is a problem, so it can be corrected before a defect occurs.

Many of the mistake-proofing examples described in this book were developed by clinicians and healthcare staff members like you. It is usually the people closest to the work who know best what problems arise and who have good ideas about how to prevent them. Since you have the most to gain from applying mistake proofing, we have developed this book specifically to give you the basics in a clear format. Once you understand these basics, you can see how they might apply to your own work situation.

One of the most effective ways to use this book is to read and discuss it with others in group learning sessions. We have planned the book so that it is easy to use in this way, with chunks of information that can be covered in a series of short sessions. (Most chapters can be covered in a single session.) Each chapter includes reflection questions to stimulate group discussion.

The mistake-proofing approach to quality is universal. Today, the basic principles of mistake proofing have been used to eliminate defects in all types of industries, and they are being put to work in healthcare organizations all over the world. We hope this book will show you how mistake proofing can make your workplace a better and safer place for both patients and staff.

Acknowledgments

We at Rona Consulting Group (RCG) and Productivity Press deeply appreciate the life work of Shigeo Shingo, developer of the ZQC system and author of *Zero Quality Control: Source Inspection and the Poka-Yoke System*. Dr. Shingo's years of observation and thinking about quality have changed the face of manufacturing around the world. We are grateful for the opportunity to share this powerful approach and its applications to healthcare services and processes.

The development of *Mistake Proofing for Lean Healthcare* has been a team effort. In particular, we would like to thank UCSF Benioff Children's Hospital Oakland, Sutter Health East Bay Region, and California Pacific Medical Center for graciously granting permission to use examples from their teams' ongoing mistake-proofing work. We would also like to acknowledge the work of John Grout and his open source wiki of mistake-proofing examples, which at the time of this writing is unfortunately no longer accessible online.

We also thank Tom Jackson, series editor; Dr. James H. Hanson and Dahlia Mak, RCG team members who enriched the book with their insights and examples; and all the RCG consultants who have contributed to our workshop "standard work." Thanks also to the team at Productivity Press and CRC Press, especially to Kristine Mednansky, Senior Editor.

Finally, we wish to acknowledge the good work of the many doctors, nurses, technicians, administrators, and executives who are now in the process of systematically mistake proofing their own healthcare processes and services. We are very pleased to bring you this addition to our Lean Tools for Healthcare Series and wish you continued and increasing success on your lean journey.

Getting Started

1.1 PURPOSE OF THIS BOOK

Mistake Proofing for Lean Healthcare was written to give you the information you need to participate in systematically preventing mistakes in your workplace. You are a valued member of your healthcare organization's transformation team; your knowledge, support, and participation are necessary to the success of any major improvement effort in your organization.

You may be reading this book because your team leader or manager asked you to do so. Or, you may be reading it because you think it will provide information that will help you in your work. By the time you finish Chapter 1, you will have a better idea of how the information in this book can help you and your healthcare organization eliminate waste and serve your patients more effectively.

1.2 WHAT THIS BOOK IS BASED ON

Mistake Proofing for Lean Healthcare is based on Shigeo Shingo's book *Zero Quality Control: Source Inspection and the Poka-Yoke System,* published in English by Productivity Press in 1986. The goal of *Zero Quality Control* (ZQC) is to provide services with zero defects.

It took Dr. Shingo 26 years to develop the ZQC system. As he studied production operations in many factories, he discovered two important facts that are the basis of ZQC:

1. No matter how good you are at finding defects, no matter how thoroughly you follow up with corrective action, improving your defect inspection

and feedback process will not prevent defects from happening in the first place.

2. To prevent defects, you must look at the process to determine what condition leads to the defect, then control that condition.

The book you are currently reading presents the main concepts and tools of Dr. Shingo's book as they are used in healthcare processes. It presents these principles in a shortened and simplified version.

1.3 TWO WAYS TO USE THIS BOOK

There are at least two ways to use this book:

1. As reading material for a learning group or study group process within your organization
2. For learning on your own

Your organization may decide to design its own learning group process based on *Mistake Proofing for Lean Healthcare*. Or, you may read this book for individual learning without formal group discussion. Either way, you will learn valuable concepts and techniques to apply in your daily work.

1.4 HOW TO GET THE MOST OUT OF YOUR READING

1.4.1 Become Familiar with This Book as a Whole

There are a few steps you can follow to make it easier to absorb the information in this book. Take as much time as you need to become familiar with the material. First, get a "big picture" view of the book by doing the following:

1. Scan the Contents to see how *Mistake Proofing for Lean Healthcare* is set up.
2. Read the rest of this chapter for an overview of the book's contents.

3. Flip through the book to get a feel for its style, flow, and design. Notice how the chapters are structured and glance at the figures.
4. Read parts of Chapter 7, Reflections and Conclusions, to obtain a sense of the book's direction.

1.4.2 Become Familiar with Each Chapter

For each chapter in *Mistake Proofing for Lean Healthcare,* we suggest you follow these steps to get the most from your reading:

1. Flip through the chapter, looking at the way it is presented.
2. Read the chapter; enhance your reading by doing the following:

   - Use the margin assists to help you follow the flow of information.
   - If the book is your own, use a highlighter to mark key information and answers to your questions about the material. If the book is not your own, take notes on a separate piece of paper.
   - Answer the Take Five questions in the text. These will help you absorb the information by reflecting on how you might apply it in your own workplace.
   - Read the summary at the end of each chapter to confirm what you have learned. If you do not remember something in the summary, find that section in the chapter and review it.
   - Finally, read the Reflections questions at the end of the chapter. Think about these questions and write down your answers.

1.4.3 Using a Reading Strategy

When reading a book, many people think they should start with the first word and read straight through to the end. This is not usually the best way to learn from a book. The method described here is easier and more effective.

Key Point
A reading strategy is based on two simple points about the way people learn. The first point is this: *It is difficult for your brain to absorb new information if it does not have a structure in which to place it.* As an analogy, imagine trying to build a house without first putting up a framework.

Like building a frame for a house, you can give your brain a framework for the new information in the book by getting an overview of the contents and then flipping through the material. Within each chapter, you repeat this process on a smaller scale by reading the key points and headings before reading the text.

Key Point
The second point about learning is this: *It is a lot easier to learn if you take in the information one layer at a time instead of trying to absorb it all at once.* It is like finishing the walls of a house: First you lay down a coat of primer. When that is dry, you apply a coat of paint and later a finish coat.

1.4.4 Using the Margin Assists

As you have noticed by now, this book uses small images called *margin assists* to help you follow the information in each chapter. There are six types of margin assists used in this book:

Background
INFO

1. **Background Information:** Sets the stage for what comes next.

Definition

2. **Definition:** Defines important words.

Key Point

3. **Key Point:** Highlights important ideas to remember.

Example

4. **Example:** Helps you understand the key points.

How-to Steps

5. **How-to Steps:** Gives you a set of directions for using new tools.

Principle

6. **Principle:** Explains how things work in a variety of situations.

1.5 OVERVIEW OF THE CONTENTS

1.5.1 Chapter 1: Getting Started

The chapter you are reading explains the purpose of *Mistake Proofing for Lean Healthcare* and how it was written. It gives tips for getting the most out of your reading and provides an overview of each chapter.

1.5.2 Chapter 2: The Production Processes and Operations of Healthcare

Chapter 2 describes the industrial origins of the lean healthcare methodology and the critical distinction between healthcare processes and operations. It also presents the five key principles of lean healthcare management.

1.5.3 Chapter 3: Introduction to Mistake Proofing

Chapter 3 introduces and defines *mistake proofing*. It also explains why focusing on zero defects is important in healthcare organizations and how mistake proofing will make your work easier, safer, and more rewarding. Finally, it explains what causes defects in the first place and how conditions can be controlled to prevent them.

1.5.4 Chapter 4: Basic Elements of the Mistake-Proofing System

Chapter 4 presents the key concept of "quality at the source" and explains the four basic elements of mistake proofing: source inspection, 100 percent inspection, quick feedback and action on problems, and "poka-yoke" or mistake-proofing methods and devices. It also gives you an overview of traditional ways of inspecting processes and products for defects and introduces you in greater detail to source inspection, an approach that catches problems before they become defects.

1.5.5 Chapter 5: Using Poka-Yoke Systems

Chapter 5 describes poka-yoke systems in detail: how they are used, how they regulate processes, types of poka-yoke systems, and types of sensing devices that are used in poka-yoke systems.

1.5.6 Chapter 6: Examples of Poka-Yoke Applications

Chapter 6 presents a number of examples of poka-yoke systems in use in healthcare. Exposure to a variety of applications will help you understand how poka-yoke systems are put to use and will give you ideas for how to apply them in your own workplace.

1.5.7 Chapter 7: Reflections and Conclusions

Chapter 7 presents reflections on and conclusions to this book. It discusses possibilities for applying what you have learned and suggests ways for you to create a personal action plan for applying mistake proofing. Finally, it describes opportunities for further learning about mistake proofing.

Chapter 2

The Production Processes and Operations of Healthcare

2.1 THE INDUSTRIAL ORIGINS OF LEAN HEALTHCARE

The purpose of the Lean Tools for Healthcare Series is to introduce readers to a set of methods that have been proven to increase patient safety and dramatically reduce the cost of providing healthcare services. The term *lean* was coined to express the notion that, like an athlete, an organization should be without organizational "fat" or what lean specialists refer to as non-value-adding waste, where *value* refers to what a patient would be willing to pay for. Figure 2.1 lists seven distinct types of waste found in healthcare.

Background INFO Lean tools and methods have important origins in the United States but were perfected principally within Toyota Motor Company between 1948 and 1963. They have since been copied by most sectors of the manufacturing industry. The first major implementation in the healthcare industry began in 2001, when Virginia Mason Medical Center in Seattle, Washington, engaged consultants (most of whom had been production engineers at Toyota and Boeing Aircraft Company) to teach them how to apply the Toyota Production System to the production of healthcare services. A few years later, another major implementation was launched by Park Nicollet Health

7 Wastes in Healthcare Operations and Administration		
Definitions	Healthcare wastes	Administrative wastes
1. Overproduction Producing more, sooner, or faster than is required by the next process.	Performing services that patients don't need or desire. Unnecessary backups between departments. Multiple quality control checks.	Printing or processing reports, emails, or other information products before they are needed. Overdissemination of reports.
2. Waiting Time delays, process idle time.	Waiting for lab results. Waiting for doctors. Waiting for nurses. Waiting for patients. Waiting for decisions from hospital administrators. Idle people.	Searching for information. Waiting for information system response. Waiting for approvals from superiors.
3. Transportation Unnecessary handling or transportation; multiple handling.	Excessive medical record pickups and deliveries. Extra hand-offs. Excess patient transfer/movement.	Transferring data files between incompatible computer systems or software packages. Overdissemination of reports.
4. Overprocessing Unnecessary processing, steps, or work elements/ procedures.	Asking the patient the same question 20 times. Multiple signatures. Extra copies of same form. Duplicate data input entries.	Re-entering data, extra copies; reformatting or excessive/custom formatting. Unnecessary reviews. CCs on emails.
5. Inventory Producing, holding, or purchasing unnecessary inventory.	Cabinets full of gloves. Piles of paper forms. Too many suture materials. Too many prosthetic devices. Multiple storage sites.	Decisions in process. Outdated, obsolete information in file cabinets or stored in databases.
6. Motion Excessive handling, unnecessary steps, nonergonomic motion.	Long reach/walk distances. Lifting more than 35 pounds. Standing all day. Sitting all day. Not enough printers. Not enough copiers.	Repetitive stress injuries resulting from poor keyboard design. Excessive walking to and from remote printers.
7. Defects Rework, correction of errors, quality problems, equipment problems.	Adverse events. High infection rates. Wrong meds. Wrong surgical site. Frequent rescheduling. Patient readmissions.	Order-entry errors. Too many bill rejects. Design errors and engineering change orders. Invoice errors. Info system downtime.

FIGURE 2.1 The seven wastes. (From J. Michael Rona and Associates, LLC, doing business as Rona Consulting Group © 2008–2015. http://www.ronaconsulting.com. All rights reserved. Reprinted with permission.)

Services in Minneapolis, Minnesota, and a few other organizations, including Thedacare in Wisconsin. The success of these implementations is well documented.[*]

Naturally, readers coming to the subject of "lean healthcare" for the first time are often perplexed by the patently industrial

---

[*] John Black with David Miller, *The Toyota Way to Healthcare Excellence: Increase Efficiency and Improve Quality with Lean* (Chicago: Health Administration Press, 2008).

point of view taken by lean healthcare specialists. How can healthcare be treated as an industrial process? Is medicine not an art? Can healthcare processes be standardized when all patients are unique? In fact, medicine and healthcare practice are generally becoming more scientific or evidence based; the Centers for Medicare and Medicaid Services (CMS) and deeming authorities such as the Joint Commission are quick to require adherence to standardized, evidence-based practices. Moreover, industrial engineering has long been applied to healthcare processes. Some readers may recall actor Clifton Webb's portrayal of the consultant Frank Gilbreth in the 1950 film *Cheaper by the Dozen*. A portion of the movie depicts Gilbreth's groundbreaking time and motion studies of surgery in hospital operating rooms. In many ways, the practice of lean healthcare continues in the tradition of Gilbreth's time studies. The major difference is that the studies are not carried out by consultants; the studies are conducted by members of the healthcare team (clinicians and support staff), frequently with the voluntary participation of patients themselves.

2.2 PRODUCTION, PROCESS, AND OPERATION

Before studying lean healthcare, you must understand precisely how the notion of "production" applies to the production of healthcare services.* As perplexing as it may seem, production is not necessarily an activity that requires machines.

Definition *Production is the making of either a product or a service— it does not matter which.* Obviously, artisans produced goods and services before the advent of steam power. In its most general sense, production is simply a network of what industrial engineers call processes and operations.

Definition *A process is a sequence of cycles of work called "operations." An operation is a work cycle defined by a sequence of component tasks.*

---

* Much of this chapter paraphrases, in language friendly to healthcare, Chapter 1 of Shigeo Shingo's groundbreaking book, *A Study of the Toyota Production System from an Industrial Engineering Perspective* (Cambridge, MA: Productivity Press, 1989).

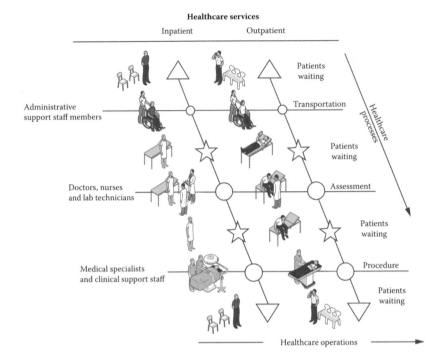

FIGURE 2.2 The healthcare service production process. (From J. Michael Rona and Associates, LLC, doing business as Rona Consulting Group, and iStockphoto LP, © 2008–2015. http://www. ronaconsulting.com. All rights reserved. Reprinted with permission.)

Figure 2.2 illustrates how a healthcare process—transforming a patient from the state of "unhealthy" to "healthy"—is accomplished through a series of medical and other healthcare operations. When we look at a healthcare process over time (especially when we see it from the patient's perspective), we see flows of patients, clinicians, medicines, supplies, equipment, and information in time and space. We see the transformation of the patient from the moment at which he or she presents undiagnosed symptoms to initial assessment, definitive diagnosis, and finally treatment and recovery. When we look at operations, on the other hand, we see the work performed by doctors, nurses, lab technicians, pharmacists, and so on to accomplish this transformation—the interaction of patients, clinicians, medications, information, supplies, and equipment in time and space.

Key Point   To make fundamental improvement in the process of producing healthcare services, we must distinguish the flow of patients (process) from the clinical work flow (operations) and analyze them separately. This is why Figure 2.2 illustrates healthcare production as a network of processes and operations. The analysis of healthcare *processes* examines the flow of patients; the analysis of healthcare *operations* examines the work performed on patients by clinicians and support staff.

Example

Consider a typical patient, a patient who makes a visit to an outpatient clinic: First, the patient registers at the front desk and then is asked to wait. Next, a medical assistant calls the patient and escorts him or her to an examination room. The medical assistant may take the patient's blood pressure and ask questions to make an initial assessment of the patient's condition. Again, the patient is asked to wait until the doctor is ready. Finally, the doctor interviews the patient and reaches a diagnosis. After this, the patient receives some treatment—say, an injection administered by a nurse, who first draws the prescribed medication and, after cleaning the patient's injection site, injects the medication into the patient. This series of changes in the patient (from undiagnosed to treated) is the process. The nurse's actions of filling the syringe, cleaning the patient's injection site, and injecting the medication into the patient constitute a single operation within the process. In the healthcare industry, such operations are often referred to as *protocols*.

2.3 PRINCIPLES OF LEAN HEALTHCARE MANAGEMENT

Definition

Lean management is the decentralized organization of management control structures to promote the discovery, correction, anticipation, and prevention of process defects and the errors and abnormalities that result in defects.

In the broadest sense, lean healthcare can be explained in terms of five principles that define what we may call the DNA of lean healthcare management:

Principle

1. Standard work
2. Autonomation

1. Standard work	All work should be organized as standardized sequences of standardized tasks performed within a standard time and supported by a standardized amount of work in process.
2. Autonomation	When defects occur, the process should stop until the defect is corrected. Where necessary, employ mistake-proofing checklists or devices to promote critical thinking about problems in the work.
3. Flow	Ideally, patients should flow through operations and processes without interruption and without waiting.
4. PDCA	When problems occur, they should be resolved *at the source* using the scientific method of PDCA (plan–do–check–act). "At the source" means close to where the problem originally occurred, which is normally far away from where it was eventually detected.
5. Socratic method	Leaders should employ the Socratic method of questioning to develop their people as scientific problem solvers.

FIGURE 2.3 Five principles of lean management.

3. Flow production
4. PDCA (plan–do–check–act)
5. Socratic method

These five principles are summarized in Figure 2.3.

2.3.1 Standard Work

Definition

The first principle of lean management is that all activity—whether clinical or administrative—is governed by means of standard work. *Standard work is defined as standardized tasks performed in a standardized sequence in a standardized amount of time and with a standardized amount of medicines, supplies, and equipment to support it.* Standard work has two functions. First, it reduces variation by bringing processes into statistical process control (i.e., the quality rate $\geq$ 3-sigma). When a process is in statistical control, the process has become predictable and we can stop fighting fires. Currently, most healthcare processes are significantly out of control at 2-sigma or probably lower. Second, standard work establishes controlled conditions for small tests of change using PDCA (see further discussion). Because controlled processes are predictable, we can concentrate on preventing defects in the future. For more information about standard work and how to implement it, see *Standard Work for Lean Healthcare* (T. L. Jackson, editor, Productivity Press, New York, 2012).

2.3.2 Autonomation

Definition

The second principle of lean management governs how different operations in a process are linked together. This principle is known as *autonomation* or, in Japanese, *jidoka*. *Autonomation is defined as stopping the process to build in quality.* Autonomation means essentially two things. First, we never send defects downstream to the next operation in the process; we must stop to fix defects immediately. Second, to increase the speed at which we discover and fix defects, we build inspection into each critical step of the process with checklists (such as the World Health Organization's Surgical Safety Checklist) and other "mistake-proofing" protocols and devices. That is the subject of this book. In all handoffs from upstream to downstream operations and processes, there must be *zero ambiguity* about what the downstream operations and processes need from the upstream operations and processes that supply them.

2.3.3 Flow Production

Definition

The third lean principle is flow production. *Flow means treating patients one at a time, with clinicians and support staff passing the patient from one step in the process to the next without inconveniencing him or her to wait or travel long distances.* Flow is always the most efficient way to deliver healthcare services. In flow, an operator (that is, a clinician or other staff member) completes work with one patient before proceeding with the next patient. A good example of flow in healthcare is the production of healthcare services for trauma victims. Flow can only happen when the downstream process serving the patient is ready. If the patient moves before that operation or process is ready, the patient will have to wait for the downstream operation. Flow is the natural outcome of eliminating the seven non-value-added wastes in Figure 2.1. It is the ideal state of an orderly production process. Think of flow as the antichaos principle.

Flow production has a corollary principle known as pull. If it is not possible for patients to flow through a healthcare process because of an acute medical condition or for any other reason, we will ask them to wait a short time, under the appropriate level of care, until the downstream process is ready to "pull" them.

2.3.4 Plan–Do–Check–Act

Chris Argyris, father of the learning organization concept, once described organizational learning as a process of detecting and correcting defects. One might say that a learning organization is an organization that finds defects and fixes them. A *lean* organization is an organization that *anticipates* defects and *prevents* them through a process of what Argyris described as "double-loop" learning. Single-loop learning is the repeated attempt to solve a problem, with no variation of method and without questioning the goal. Double-loop learning is the ability to modify organizational methods or even goals in the light of experience. The method by which double-loop learning is accomplished within the lean enterprise is the scientific method, summarized by the Deming cycle, or PDCA.* We explore the PDCA cycle in more depth in Chapter 3.

2.3.5 Socratic Method

The fifth and final lean principle is the Socratic method. Lean processes are highly—some say *radically*—decentralized. To

---

* For Argyris's comments about detecting and correcting defects, see M. Crossan, "Altering Theories of Learning and Action: An Interview with Chris Argyris," *Academy of Management Executive* 17(2):40 (2003). On double-loop learning, see Chris Argyris and Dan Schön, *Organizational Learning: A Theory of Action Perspective* (Reading, MA: Addison-Wesley, 1978).

fix defects and maintain flow, clinicians and support staff must be both qualified and empowered to make decisions in real time. Otherwise, the time between discovery and correction of defects will grow indefinitely as permission to change the process is chased up the chain of command. Obviously, this cannot be done without support from leaders, but that goes beyond management support in the traditional sense. In a lean organization, leaders must be teachers who have mastered what is perhaps the most demanding and effective teaching method ever conceived: the Socratic method. Teachers (sometimes called *sensei*) use the Socratic method to encourage students to develop their own problem-solving powers by posing a series of open-ended questions rather than giving answers.

2.4 SUMMARY

All healthcare production carried out in any healthcare setting—in the operating room, the clinic, the lab, or the pharmacy—must be understood as a functional network of process and operation. Healthcare processes transform unwell patients into well patients. Healthcare operations are the clinical actions that accomplish those transformations. These fundamental concepts and their relationship must be understood to make effective, evidence-based improvements in the production of healthcare services.

Lean management, which involves decentralized management control structures designed to prevent errors and defects, is based on five key principles: standard work, autonomation, flow, PDCA, and the Socratic method.

2.5 REFLECTIONS

Now that you have completed this chapter, take 5 minutes to think about these questions and write down your answers:

- What did you learn from reading this chapter that stands out as being particularly useful or interesting to you in healthcare?

- How do you feel about the idea of "producing" health-care services using industrial methods?
- Do you have any questions about the topics presented in this chapter? If so, what are they?
- Are there any special obstacles in your mind or the minds of your colleagues to applying the distinction between process and operation or the five key principles of lean management in healthcare?
- What information do you still need to fully understand the ideas presented?
- How can you obtain this information?
- Whom do you need to involve in this process?

Chapter 3

Introduction to Mistake Proofing

3.1 WHAT IS MISTAKE PROOFING?

Definition

Mistake proofing is an approach for achieving defect-free services and products. It is based on a quality system known as Zero Quality Control (ZQC).* *Zero* refers to the goal of this approach: to make products and deliver services with zero defects. In other words, it is a way of building quality into processes or integrating quality directly into standard work. It is a core element of autonomation, the second principle of lean management (see Chapter 2).

Principle

Mistake proofing (or ZQC) is based on the principle that defects are prevented by controlling the performance of a process so that it cannot produce defects—even when a person or piece of equipment makes an error or mistake.

We use mistake proofing to get beyond blaming people as the main course of action when an error occurs. To prevent mistakes from recurring, we need to be able to see them. Finger-pointing does nothing to help us see mistakes; in fact, it drives mistakes underground. When we systematically make processes mistake proof, on the other hand, we take into account the fact that equipment and people make mistakes sometimes. We study how mistakes occur and build in ways to keep *errors* from turning into *defects*.

Definition

A mistake or error is something done incorrectly, through a misunderstanding or as a result of an unreliable or unstable process, and not corrected. An error is

---

* The term *mistake proofing* is used throughout to refer to the ZQC system.

likely to occur when any of the conditions necessary for successful processing are wrong or absent. The resulting departure from correct performance causes a *defect.*

A *defect* is a nonconformance or departure from expected quality. It is the result of an uncorrected human error or equipment malfunction that has been passed on undetected from one worker to the next. Errors become defects *when they start to travel.*

An *abnormality* is any process or equipment condition that does not conform to the standard conditions required for the scheduled delivery of quality healthcare services. Examples of abnormal conditions include incorrect information, substandard environmental conditions, and equipment malfunctions.

In the following chapters, you will learn how mistake proofing works. You will also learn why it is important and how it can help your healthcare workplace be safer, more efficient, and more effective—and therefore more satisfying for both patients and staff.

3.2 WHY FOCUS ON ZERO DEFECTS?

One important reason for producing defect-free healthcare services is to maintain patient safety. Healthcare defects are a significant factor in avoidable patient injury and death. In keeping with the long-standing healthcare principle of "first, do no harm," getting to zero defects is a core responsibility of those entrusted with the lives and health of patients. Patient safety also affects the staff's sense of teamwork and engagement. In addition to hurting patients, harm events damage morale.

Another important reason for producing defect-free services is to maintain patient satisfaction and loyalty. Even one defective service can cause significant patient dissatisfaction and damage a healthcare provider's reputation. As hospital safety data become more readily available to the public, provider ratings will affect more patients' choices of where to receive care.

Cost is another reason to produce defect-free services. A defect always costs something, whether it is the expense of throwing away supplies, redoing work, repairing equipment damage, or paying more for malpractice insurance. Fixing defects in processes requires more resources. Avoidable complications may not be reimbursed. And, even when no patient injury has occurred, rework to fix defects requires human hours and effort that could be better spent on value-added activities.

Key Point   Finally, *targeting zero defects is a key factor in a health-care organization's ability to adopt lean production methods with just-in-time provision of services and smaller inventories.* Many healthcare organizations maintain excess supplies and resources as a buffer to avoid problems when mistakes happen or defects occur. Mistake proofing ensures that processes work correctly the first time, which allows a healthcare organization to provide only the services that are required by and are value added for patients.

3.3 HOW MISTAKE PROOFING MAKES WORK EASIER

Key Point   We do not talk about "foolproofing" the process, we talk about "mistake proofing" it. That is because *it is natural for people to make mistakes* or not to notice when an error is made or equipment acts up—it does not mean a person is stupid or foolish.

Key Point   Mistake proofing has nothing to do with pointing fingers after the fact or hassling people to "do better next time." *Instead, to achieve zero defects we use mistake-proofing protocols and devices that keep errors from ever turning into defects.*

Producing services without defects means less rework and less additional effort. Zero-defect processes support you and your healthcare organization's reputation for providing high-quality care. They keep patients and staff safe and satisfied, let you spend more time on value-added work for patients, and help keep costs low.

Clinicians and staff members play an important role in reaching the zero-defects goal. Most of the mistake-proofing examples you will read about in this book were implemented by teams of clinicians and staff members.

3.4 WHAT CAUSES DEFECTS?

Background
INFO Most defects happen in one of five situations:

1. Inappropriate or inadequate procedures or standards are specified when the process is planned, or standards are lacking.
2. Excessive variability happens during service operations or processes. Of course, "necessary variation" is the art of medicine: Healthcare providers must know how to apply a standard approach to treatment while taking into account the unique needs and situations of individual patients. "Unnecessary variation" stems from the lack of a standard approach or the use of different standards by different people.
3. Damaged or excessively variable supplies are used.
4. Inadequately maintained tools and equipment cause problems.
5. Finally, even when the first four situations are just right, human errors occur or tasks are carried out imperfectly.

The first four situations can be predicted, and countermeasures can be implemented to avoid these sources of defects.

Key Point *But, human errors—the most frequent cause of defects in all human activity, including healthcare—can seem to occur unpredictably.* This makes them harder to prevent.

If we understand the conditions that can make human errors more likely to occur, we can take measures to prevent them. Three concepts that help us understand the nature of human mistakes are *communication errors, cognitive errors,* and *red-flag conditions.*

3.4.1 Communication Errors

Key Point *Communication is one of the most frequently named root causes contributing to sentinel events.*[*] Communication errors often occur during patient handoffs. Therefore, it is essential

---

[*] Joint Commission. "Sentinel Event Data: Root Causes by Event Type, 2004–2Q 2014." http://www.jointcommission.org/Sentinel_Event_Statistics/ (accessed February 19, 2015).

to ensure that information passed during handoffs is error free and unambiguous.

When an error in communication occurs at one point in a process or at one handoff, it will spread downstream to subsequent operations and processes unless we catch it. As it moves, a simple communication error can cause more and more problems and result in serious defects. And, with increasing use of electronic medical records and the cut-and-paste function in software, it becomes easier and easier for mistakes in communication to proliferate rapidly throughout the healthcare system.

3.4.2 Cognitive Errors

Definition

Cognitive errors are thinking errors that can occur when we use intuitive thought processes in decision making. The use of "expert intuition" and mental shortcuts (or heuristics) is unavoidable. In fact, these are critical and appropriate parts of the way we function. But, they can also lead us to mistakes in judgment. There are many examples of competent, credible people getting caught up in a thinking error that resulted in defects and patient harm. Some common types of cognitive errors are listed in Figure 3.1.[*]

Key Point

We are all prone to falling into these traps in patterns of thought. But, with increased awareness of different types of cognitive errors, *we can learn to step back in some situations and activate a more deliberate and analytical form of thinking* that can help us avoid mistakes.

Team approaches to service production and improvement also help by bringing the benefit of multiple sets of eyes to review operations and processes. Patients and their families can also be drawn into the loop by asking them: "Does this make sense to you?"

3.4.3 Red-Flag Conditions

Definition

Certain environmental conditions are known to trigger human error. *These high-risk, high-volume, or problem-prone situations*

---

[*] For more information on cognitive errors, see the books by Daniel Kahneman and Jerome Groopman listed in the Appendix.

Cognitive Errors

Availability	A mental shortcut relying on immediate examples that come to mind. "What you see is what you know."
Confirmation bias	The tendency for people to prefer information that confirms their preconceptions or hypotheses, independently of whether they are true or not.
Anchoring	The common human tendency to rely too heavily, or "anchor," on one trait or piece of information when making decisions.
Diagnostic momentum	A prevalent error, where the very first diagnosis made by the primary care physician sends all subsequent specialists taking care of the patient down the wrong path.
Order effects	In transitions of care, some information is given too much or too little consideration because of the order in which it was presented.
Premature closure	When the diagnosis is made, the thinking stops.

Figure 3.1 Several common types of cognitive errors.

Red-Flag Conditions

1. Multiple processes, steps, or inputs—too much information (TMI), noisiness, chaos
2. High volume
3. Infrequent production or use of a process, equipment, or supplies
4. Critical symmetry/asymmetry configurations
5. Revisions or changes
6. Repetitive, fast-paced operations
7. Critical conditions, orders, or specifications
8. Poorly maintained equipment or tools
9. Ineffective standard procedures or processes
10. New people, processes, or services
11. Multiple suppliers
12. Shortcuts and workarounds
13. Same information in numerous places
14. Poor environmental conditions
15. Fatigue
16. Interruptions

Figure 3.2 Common red-flag conditions in healthcare.

are referred to as red-flag conditions. Some examples of red-flag conditions are shown in Figure 3.2. When we recognize red-flag conditions, we can work to improve and mistake-proof operations and processes that take place under those conditions.

Key Point

Because the goal of mistake proofing is to *prevent all defects,* not just to reduce the number of defects, *mistake-proofing systems provide a way to catch mistakes before they turn into defects.* They rely on a control function that ensures the necessary conditions are present to produce defect-free services. The next section describes more about the control function used in mistake proofing.

TAKE FIVE

Take a few minutes to think about these questions and to write down your answers:

- What problems or frustrations do you experience in your work as a result of defects that occur?
- What kinds of things can cause defects to happen in your process?
- Can you describe some instances when communication errors, cognitive errors, or red-flag conditions caused errors or mistakes in your process?

3.5 CONTROLLING CONDITIONS SO DEFECTS DO NOT HAPPEN

3.5.1 The Traditional Quality Improvement Cycle

Background
INFO

The PDCA cycle shown in Figure 3.3 is often emphasized in traditional quality improvement activities. In this cycle, optimal processing conditions are established in the "plan" phase. The planned actions then take place in the "do" phase. Quality monitoring is performed in the "check" phase. Finally, countermeasures and improvements to correct process problems are addressed in the "act" phase. If a defect is found, the information is fed back and corrective action is taken in the next plan phase to improve processing conditions for the next do phase.

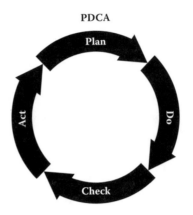

Figure 3.3 Traditional plan–do–check–act (PDCA) cycle.

Continuously repeating the functions in this cycle will lead to higher levels of quality. This cycle alone, however, can never completely prevent defects, especially those caused by human errors or machine mistakes. *The PDCA cycle does not provide a way to catch errors; it gives feedback only after an actual defect happens.*

Key Point

It is important to remember that an error is not the same as a defect. An error is what happens to *cause* the defect. Rather than detecting defects that have already happened, the trick is to catch the error before it turns into a defect. Mistake proofing solves this problem by embedding a kind of automatic PDCA cycle within the do phase to ensure that the plan is properly carried out.

3.5.2 Integrating PDCA in the Mistake-Proofing Approach

Unpredictable errors can creep in between the plan and do functions. Something happens and the plan is not carried out properly. That is why *the mistake-proofing approach integrates a reflexive check phase, or PDCA cycle, during the do phase,* so that quality is checked and ensured at the point where problems arise. This is an essential part of building in quality or *ensuring quality at the source.* The mistake-proofing quality cycle is shown in Figure 3.4.

Key Point

We embed this mistake-proofing quality cycle directly into standard work by using what we call *source inspection—*a

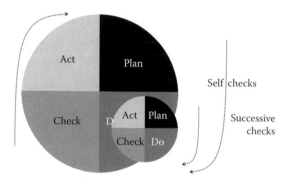

Figure 3.4 Mistake-proofing quality cycle.

check for proper processing conditions that is made before the processing is done. When a manager or staff member detects an error (an operating condition that is not as it should be, for instance), he or she corrects it before work is completed and passed on to the next operation. Source inspection provides instant feedback so that problems can be corrected *before* defects happen, not after.

The mistake-proofing approach is made up of four basic elements: *source inspection, 100 percent inspection, a short feedback loop,* and *mistake-proofing devices and protocols* called *poka-yoke* (pronounced POH-kah YOK-kay). It also includes the use of *self-checks* as well as *successive checks* (checks by the next person or operation in a process). These types of checks speed up the process of catching and correcting mistakes and defects when they do occur. Chapter 4 describes the elements of a mistake-proofing system in more detail.

3.6 SUMMARY

Mistake proofing, or the ZQC system, is an approach for achieving zero defects. Mistake proofing is based on the principle that defects can be prevented by controlling the performance of a process so that it cannot produce defects, even when a person or machine makes a mistake.

There are several key reasons for focusing on zero-defect services. The first is to maintain the safety of patients and staff. Another is to maintain patient satisfaction and loyalty. Zero-defect processes also prevent the unnecessary costs of rework and downtime. And, striving for zero defects is a key factor in a healthcare organization's ability to adopt lean production methods with just-in-time provision of services and smaller inventories of supplies.

We do not talk about foolproofing the process; we talk about mistake-proofing it. Rather than pointing fingers after the fact or hassling people to do better next time, we use mistake-proofing protocols and devices to keep errors from ever turning into defects in the first place.

Defects are most often caused by (1) specification of inappropriate procedures or standards; (2) excessive variability in processes; (3) damaged or excessively variable supplies; (4) inadequately maintained tools and equipment; or (5) human errors or tasks that are imperfectly carried out.

Human errors are the most common cause of defects, and they are the hardest to prevent. It can help to recognize that errors happen frequently during communication and hand-offs, at times when we are prone to mistakes in cognition, and under red-flag conditions. Because the goal of mistake proofing is to prevent all defects, however, errors must be caught. This is done by way of a control function that ensures that the necessary conditions are present to produce defect-free services.

The traditional quality improvement cycle is the PDCA cycle. This cycle catches and corrects defects after they occur, but it does not ensure that work is done according to plan in the first place. Mistake proofing embeds a kind of automatic PDCA cycle or check phase within the do phase. This gives instant feedback so problems can be corrected *before* defects happen.

3.7 REFLECTIONS

Now that you have completed this chapter, take 5 minutes to think about these questions and to write down your answers:

- What did you learn from reading this chapter that stands out as particularly useful or interesting?

- Do you have any questions about the topics presented in this chapter? If so, what are they?
- What information do you still need to fully understand the ideas presented in this chapter?
- How can you obtain this information?

Chapter 4

Basic Elements of the Mistake-Proofing System

4.1 QUALITY AT THE SOURCE

Background INFO

With the mistake-proofing system, we clearly recognize that "to err is human." The real problem is letting errors turn into defects. At worst (but as is often the case), the first time we hear about a problem is when the patient or customer complains. In effect, that patient or customer becomes the "quality or safety inspector" who has uncovered the defect, as shown in Figure 4.1. A patient or customer who has received a defective service or product is 100 percent dissatisfied and perhaps harmed.

Allowing patients to become the "inspectors" of healthcare services creates enormous costs. The cost of poor quality grows exponentially—by a factor of 10 or more—as defects travel from their source. As described in Chapter 3, poor quality also takes a toll on a provider's reputation, staff morale, malpractice insurance costs, and much more.

P

Principle

Instead, we must build quality into operations and processes to prevent errors or discover them at their source. This is the *autonomation* or *jidoka* principle of lean management, discussed in Chapter 2. It is also known as *quality at the source.*

Other lean principles and practices are foundational in establishing defect-free processes. *Visual management*

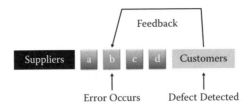

Figure 4.1 The patient or customer as "quality inspector."

and 5S* help make it easy to spot errors, defects, and abnormalities at a glance. *Standard work* helps to establish predictable processes and sets up the controlled conditions that form the baseline for improvement. Mistake proofing builds on these, providing another level of control to prevent errors and defects.

4.2 THE FOUR ELEMENTS OF MISTAKE PROOFING

Background
INFO

Recall from Chapter 3 that mistake proofing prevents defects by integrating a kind of plan–do–check–act (PDCA) or "check" cycle in the "do" phases of work. It does this by combining four basic elements:

Key Point

1. It uses *source inspection* to catch errors before they become defects.
2. It uses *100 percent inspection* to check all services, not just a sample.
3. It provides *immediate feedback,* thereby shortening the time for corrective action.
4. It uses *poka-yoke* (mistake-proofing) protocols and devices wherever possible to carry out the checking function because smart people do make mistakes.

Definition

The first element, source inspection, is the key to the mistake-proofing control function. Source inspection *ensures that the conditions necessary to perform a process properly are in place beforehand.*

---

* 5S is a disciplined approach to managing workplace organization to make it easy to identify errors, defects, abnormal conditions, and so on. The five S's are *sort, set in order, shine, standardize,* and *sustain.*

Source inspection is different from other types of quality inspection you may be familiar with. To understand how source inspection works, let us first look at how two more traditional types of quality inspection work: *judgment inspection* and *informative inspection.*

4.3 THREE APPROACHES TO INSPECTION

Background
INFO
There are three basic approaches to the inspection of products and services (see Figure 4.2):

1. Inspection that *discovers* defects: *judgment inspection*
2. Inspection that *reduces* defects: *informative inspection*
3. Inspection that *eliminates* defects: *source inspection*

Key Point
The first two approaches are common in traditional quality control. *Only the third approach—source inspection—actually eliminates defects.* It is important to understand the different approaches to inspection and what they do and do not do. The following sections describe traditional inspections and source inspection in more detail.

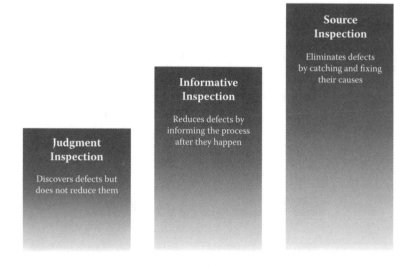

Figure 4.2 Three approaches to inspection and their results.

4.4 JUDGMENT INSPECTIONS REVEAL DEFECTS

At many organizations, *quality assurance* means a type of inspection to catch defective products or services before they reach the patient or customer. The simplest approach to this is called *judgment inspection.*

Definition

In a judgment inspection, a person or machine compares a product or service against a standard, discovers items that do not conform, and rejects them as defects (see Figure 4.3).

Example

Here is a simple example: A checker on a food tray line who sorts incorrectly assembled or "defective" food trays from correctly assembled or "good" trays, based on a standard, is performing a judgment inspection. The defective trays might be replaced, but there is no built-in way of providing feedback to prevent the food tray assembly process from preparing more defective trays in the future.

Of course, this is better than allowing defects to go out the door undetected to the patient. But, adding the inspection operation ("e" in Figure 4.3) also adds cost to the process. It is waste, as opposed to producing a service right the first time.

Key Point

Judgment inspection does not reduce the number of defects. There are two reasons for this:

1. Judgment inspection reveals defects only after they have been made. It does not prevent the defects from occurring.
2. Judgment inspection generally happens at the end of a process or after several operations have been completed. This means that there are built-in delays in the time it takes to discover a defect. In the meantime, the process may be creating more defective services. Sometimes, this information never gets back to the place where the problem began.

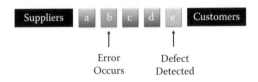

Figure 4.3 Judgment inspection.

TAKE FIVE

Take a few minutes to think about these questions and to write down your answers:

- What are the four basic elements of mistake proofing? What role does each element play in avoiding defects?
- What is judgment inspection? Does this type of inspection occur in your workplace? When is it done?

4.5 INFORMATIVE INSPECTIONS REDUCE DEFECTS

Definition
Informative inspections overcome some of the problems of judgment inspections by giving feedback to the process that produces the defect. In an informative inspection, the focus is on alerting the defect-producing process (whether it be the work of a clinician, administrator, technician, other staff member, or piece of equipment) about the problem as quickly as possible so that the problem can be corrected.

There are three ways to perform an informative inspection:

1. Statistical quality control (SQC)
2. Successive check of each service or product
3. Self-check of each service or product

Informative inspections help reduce defects, but they do not prevent them entirely. The next sections describe how the three types of informative inspection work.

4.5.1 Statistical Quality Control

The SQC approach to inspection is to check samples of a product or service after processing to determine whether they are acceptable. When a sample shows a problem, information is fed back to the process so that the problem can be corrected (see Figure 4.4). Usually, a control chart is made to track the results of this checking over time.

33

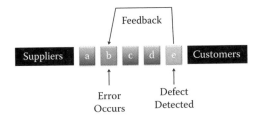

Figure 4.4 Informative inspection, such as statistical quality control.

Example

For example, a healthcare provider might randomly select patient charts on a monthly basis, audit them for incidences of preventable harm, and track and use the information to make process improvements.

Statistical quality control is better than judgment inspection because it systematically monitors and gives information back to the process. It can drive continuous improvement. However, because SQC relies on sampling rather than checking every service or product, it does not ensure 100 percent quality. It is still labor intensive, and although information is tracked, feedback and corrective action are often slow.

4.5.2 Successive Checks

Definition

One way to improve SQC inspections is to use successive checks. *In a successive check, people in the next process inspect the work that is passed to them from the previous process.* If they find a defect, they tell the previous person right away so that it can be corrected before too many more defects occur (see Figure 4.5).

Example

A simple example of a successive check would be a pharmacy technician mixing a medication, followed by a pharmacist checking the medication and providing feedback to the

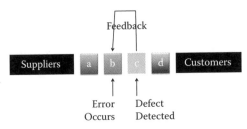

Figure 4.5 Successive checks.

technician before releasing the medication to the patient or hospital floor.

Example

Successive checks can and should be done in series. For example, a resident writes a medication order; an attending physician checks the order; a unit clerk enters the order into a computer system; a pharmacist reviews the order; a technician prepares the medication; the pharmacist checks the medication; the floor nurse confirms the medication against the order before administering it to the patient. In each case, feedback is given to the previous person in the process as needed. Successive checks and quick feedback are much easier when operators are working close to one another.

4.5.3 Self-Checks

Definition

Feedback and corrections can happen even more quickly when operators do self-checks. *In a self-check, the clinician, technician, or other staff member checks his or her own work against an appropriate standard or source document before passing it on to the next operation or process* (see Figure 4.6).

In healthcare, self-checks can help catch errors before they become defects. For example, if Nurse A did not elevate the head of the bed in the intensive care unit after bathing a patient but caught it right away and fixed it, that could be considered an error, not a defect. If Nurse B had to adjust the head of the bed or if Nurse A had to return to fix it, the error would have become a defect. But, technically, any time an error leads to an inappropriate result, a defect has already been created. So, self-checks also help catch defects that can be corrected immediately.

Self-checks give quicker feedback than successive checks; however, they cannot catch all the errors or defects. We are only human, after all, and sometimes it is hard to see our

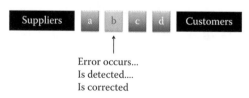

Figure 4.6 Self-checks.

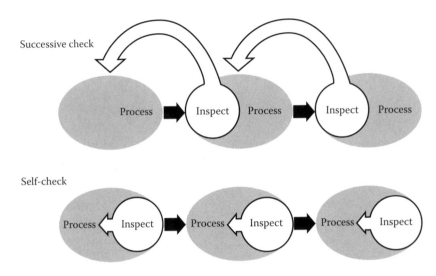

Figure 4.7 Successive checks and self-checks are types of informative inspection that give quick feedback about defects.

own mistakes as easily as someone else can. As a result, sometimes we miss things, and errors travel to the next operation or process and become defects.

As you have learned, the self-check is the most effective type of informative inspection in terms of how quickly the information gets back to the place where the error or defect occurred (see Figure 4.7).

Both self-checks and successive checks, combined with standard work and visual controls, can be effective countermeasures to prevent mistakes in healthcare processes. Unlike SQC, they can also be used to check every service or product produced. *Notice, however, that in all three types of informative inspection people are generally dealing with defects after they occur, not reliably preventing them in the first place.* The only kind of inspection that can actually prevent defects is source inspection.

Key Point

TAKE FIVE

Take a few minutes to think about these questions and to write down your answers:

- How does an informative inspection differ from a judgment inspection?

- What are the three types of informative inspection? Do you use any of these in your process?
- Which types of informative inspections do you think would be most useful in your process?

4.6 SOURCE INSPECTION KEEPS ERRORS FROM BECOMING DEFECTS

Key Point

Source inspection is one of the four basic elements of the mistake-proofing system. Source inspection differs from judgment inspection and informative inspection in a big way: It inspects the conditions for work rather than finished work. That means, *it catches errors—and gives feedback about them—before they happen or before processing, so the errors do not turn into defects.* This is the integration of the check and do phases: Something controls the "doing" so that it cannot be done wrong (see Figure 4.8).

Example

Source inspection often involves the use of poka-yoke devices (see Section 4.9) to automatically "inspect" the conditions in which a process is to be performed. For example, a switch that halts a piece of equipment if it is improperly positioned is performing a source inspection. So is a pin configuration or shape that physically prevents connecting a line incorrectly. Source inspection might also involve a warning light or sound. Such a signal can warn, for example,

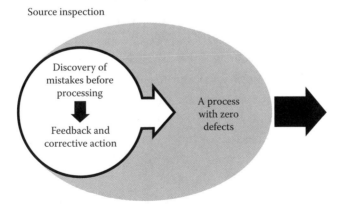

Figure 4.8 Source inspection keeps errors from turning into defects.

37

if an operation is attempted before a piece of equipment has reached proper operating conditions (such as temperature).

In processes that involve physical objects or equipment, we can frequently build in source inspection using mistake-proofing devices. More often than not, in healthcare, we must rely on human beings to have the discipline to *stop the process* to prevent an error from becoming a defect.

4.7 100 PERCENT INSPECTION CATCHES ALL ERRORS

Key Point

The second unique element of the mistake-proofing system is that it performs a source inspection on every single iteration of a service process or every product produced. This is different from SQC inspections, which usually rely on inspecting only a sampling.

Although statistical sample-checking methods can track whether a process is in control, they neither prevent defects nor guarantee that only a statistical number of defects will occur. Furthermore, SQC methods assume that a certain level of defects is unavoidable. This is inconsistent with the goal of zero defects, so mistake proofing relies on 100 percent inspection.

4.8 A SHORT FEEDBACK LOOP MEANS QUICKER ACTION ON PROBLEMS

Key Point

The third element of mistake proofing is quick feedback so that errors can be corrected right away. Traditional inspection methods do not do this very well. They happen after the process, when errors have already turned into defects. In the case of judgment inspections, the process that made the bad services may not even be informed of the defects. When it is, as in informative inspections, time has already passed. By then, the process may have churned out more defects or the conditions that caused the initial defect no longer exist and cannot be used for learning.

Successive checks and self-checks can detect defects quickly and enable speedy PDCA cycles. But, to achieve zero defects through mistake proofing, source inspection is carried out by a system that signals people about mistakes and machine errors *before* they become defects.

4.9 POKA-YOKE SYSTEMS CATCH ERRORS WE MIGHT HAVE MISSED

Key Point

The fourth element that is unique to the mistake-proofing approach is the use of *poka-yoke* systems. Rather than relying on clinicians and staff to catch their own errors or those of the previous process, *poka-yoke protocols and devices perform source inspections and give quick feedback 100 percent of the time.* They supplement standard work, successive checks, self-checks, and visual controls.

Definition

Poka-yoke systems warn and control. They warn through the use of *andons—lights, sounds, or other devices that signal the presence of defects, errors, and abnormalities.* They may also use a method or protocol (e.g., a surgical checklist review process) to signal an error, defect, or abnormality. Checklists have become critical poka-yoke methods in healthcare. They control by preventing defects from occurring and by preventing them from moving to the next process.

The best ideas for how to apply poka-yoke often come from the people who work in the process. Chapter 5 describes different types of poka-yoke systems and provides ideas for how to use them in your workplace.

TAKE FIVE

Take a few minutes to think about these questions and to write down your answers:

- How does source inspection differ from traditional types of inspection?
- How might you use source inspection and the other three elements of mistake proofing to prevent defects in your workplace?

4.10 SUMMARY

Mistake proofing supports the autonomation or jidoka principle of lean management—building quality into operations and processes and preventing errors or discovering them at their source. This is also known as *quality at the source.* Mistake proofing builds on other lean principles, including visual management, 5S, and standard work, providing another level of control to prevent errors and defects.

Mistake proofing prevents defects by combining four basic but unique approaches: source inspection, 100 percent inspection, immediate feedback, and the use of poka-yoke systems.

There are three types of inspection: judgment inspection, informative inspection, and source inspection. In judgment inspection, a person or machine compares a product or service with a standard after it has been produced, discovers items that do not conform, and rejects them as defects. In informative inspection, the focus is on informing the defect-producing process of a problem so that countermeasures can be taken. There are three types of informative inspection: SQC, successive checks, and self-checks. Successive checks and self-checks provide faster feedback than SQC and can be used to check all products or services rather than just a sample.

Source inspection, the first element of mistake proofing, catches equipment and people errors and gives feedback about them *before* processing so errors do not turn into defects.

The second element of mistake proofing is 100 percent inspection. That means that a source inspection takes place on every single product or service produced, not just a statistical sampling. The third element of mistake proofing is quick feedback so that errors can be corrected right away, not after the process has churned out more defects or the conditions that caused the initial defect no longer exist and are no longer useful for learning.

Finally, the fourth element of mistake proofing is the use of poka-yoke systems. Rather than relying on people to catch their own errors or those of the previous process, poka-yoke devices and protocols can be set up to detect errors people might have missed.

4.11 REFLECTIONS

Now that you have completed this chapter, take 5 minutes to think about these questions and to write down your answers:

- What did you learn from reading this chapter that stands out as particularly useful or interesting?
- Do you have any questions about the topics presented in this chapter? If so, what are they?
- What information do you still need to fully understand the ideas presented in this chapter?

Chapter 5

Using Poka-Yoke Systems

5.1 ABOUT POKA-YOKE SYSTEMS

Background INFO Poka-yoke systems provide a way to embed a kind of "memory" into processes, an automatic way of remembering the right, defect-free way to do something. They are used to carry out two key elements of mistake proofing: 100 percent inspection and quick feedback for corrective action.

Poka-yoke can involves tools such as checklists that are designed into the standard work for processes; sensors or devices installed in equipment and facilities; and warning systems that alert people to problems. They help to detect errors and defects that might otherwise slip by a clinician or staff member (see Figure 5.1). When a poka-yoke system detects an error or defect, it automatically shuts down equipment or gives a warning to correct the error or stop the process. How effective it is depends on whether it is used in combination with source inspection or with informative inspection (self-checks and successive checks).

5.2 POKA-YOKE SYSTEMS IN SOURCE INSPECTION AND INFORMATIVE INSPECTION (SELF-CHECKS AND SUCCESSIVE CHECKS)

Key Point *Poka-yoke systems are most effective when they are applied in source inspections* to catch errors before they occur or before they become defects. This is the only way to achieve zero defects.

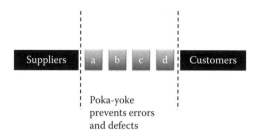

Figure 5.1 Poka-yoke systems automatically detect and prevent errors and defects.

Key Point *Poka-yoke systems can also be used in informative inspections—that is, either with self-checks or with successive checks* at the next process. Because the feedback and action generally take place after a defect has occurred, this approach will not eliminate all defects.[*] But, it can keep defects from being passed down the line, and it reduces defects more effectively than statistical sampling or no feedback at all.

This chapter describes various types of poka-yoke systems, the main approaches to using them, and some different types of sensing devices that can be used to detect abnormalities. Chapter 6 provides more specific examples of poka-yoke applications in healthcare operations and processes, including several ideas for visual control techniques that help with error proofing.

5.3 HOW POKA-YOKE SYSTEMS REGULATE THE PROCESS

Poka-yoke systems regulate processes and prevent defects by using one of two approaches:

Definition

1. A *control system* stops a process, operation, or piece of equipment when an irregularity happens.

Definition

2. A *warning system* signals the operator to stop the process or equipment or address the problem.

---

[*] As discussed in Chapter 4, self-checks can also sometimes catch errors so that they can be corrected before they truly become defects.

Key Point *A control system is more certain as a zero-defects method because it does not depend on the worker.* The equipment or process stops itself when it detects a problem. Feedback and action are required before the process can resume. However, it is not always possible or convenient to set up a control system that stops equipment or a process automatically. In such cases, a *warning or alarm system is used to get a person's attention to halt the process and fix the problem.* (Control systems also use light and sound signals because attention is needed to correct the problem.)

Example For example, a flashing light or a sound—such as an alarm that beeps or triggers a call light when there is a problem with an intravenous line—is a type of warning system. Color coding of supplies, equipment, or high-risk patients is a kind of visual control that also functions as a warning system. Color coding can be effective in catching errors before they become defects.

Because healthcare processes often involve a great deal of human interaction, it can be difficult to set up control systems that eliminate all possibility of defects. But, we can vastly improve performance and even approach zero-defect levels through poka-yoke systems that help *prevent* errors and defects and that *warn or signal* about errors or defects.

TAKE FIVE

Take a few minutes to think about these questions and to write down your answers:

- How does a poka-yoke system work?
- Why are control systems more certain to prevent defects than warning systems?

5.4 TYPES OF POKA-YOKE SYSTEMS

There are two main classes of poka-yoke systems used in healthcare and four main types of error-proofing techniques:

1. Method poka-yoke. These are typically *checklist* driven.
2. Physical poka-yoke. These involve three main types:
   a. *Contact* or *identification* techniques
   b. *Fixed-value* or *number* techniques
   c. *Motion-step* or *sequence* techniques

Method poka-yoke uses warning systems to identify errors and stop them from becoming defects. Each of the physical poka-yoke techniques can use either control systems or warning systems to regulate the process. Each technique uses a different approach for dealing with abnormalities. Think about these different approaches as you consider what kind of system would prevent defects in your particular processes.

5.5 METHOD POKA-YOKE

Definition

Method poka-yoke involves routines designed into processes to mistake proof them. In healthcare, method poka-yoke systems typically involve the use of checklists at appropriate points of critical processes (particularly in situations where significant patient harm may occur). An entire process may also be represented as a checklist. Whether manual or computer driven, checklists provide a warning system to alert people about potential errors and defects.

Background
INFO

Pilots involved in flight-testing new aircraft began to use checklists in the 1930s to help them perform complicated arrays of tasks. These highly trained pilots found that a simple checklist dramatically reduced errors and improved safety.

5.5.1 Checklists in Healthcare

Checklists are increasingly being adopted to prevent errors and defects in healthcare, especially in efforts to prevent CLABSI (central line-associated bloodstream infection) and in surgical units. Figure 5.2 shows a surgical safety checklist developed by the World Health Organization (WHO). It is a template that can be adapted for specific surgical settings.

Surgical Safety Checklist

World Health Organization | Patient Safety
A World Alliance for Safer Health Care

Before induction of anaesthesia

(with at least nurse and anaesthetist)

Has the patient confirmed his/her identity, site, procedure, and consent?
☐ Yes

Is the site marked?
☐ Yes
☐ Not applicable

Is the anaesthesia machine and medication check complete?
☐ Yes

Is the pulse oximeter on the patient and functioning?
☐ Yes

Does the patient have a:

Known allergy?
☐ No
☐ Yes

Difficult airway or aspiration risk?
☐ No
☐ Yes, and equipment/assistance available

Risk of >500ml blood loss (7ml/kg in children)?
☐ No
☐ Yes, and two IVs/central access and fluids planned

Before skin incision

(with nurse, anaesthetist and surgeon)

Confirm all team members have introduced themselves by name and role.

Confirm the patient's name, procedure, and where the incision will be made.

Has antibiotic prophylaxis been given within the last 60 minutes?
☐ Yes
☐ Not applicable

Anticipated Critical Events

To Surgeon:
☐ What are the critical or non-routine steps?
☐ How long will the case take?
☐ What is the anticipated blood loss?

To Anaesthetist:
☐ Are there any patient-specific concerns?

To Nursing Team:
☐ Has sterility (including indicator results) been confirmed?
☐ Are there equipment issues or any concerns?

Is essential imaging displayed?
☐ Yes
☐ Not applicable

Before patient leaves operating room

(with nurse, anaesthetist and surgeon)

Nurse Verbally Confirms:
☐ The name of the procedure
☐ Completion of instrument, sponge and needle counts
☐ Specimen labelling (read specimen labels aloud, including patient name)
☐ Whether there are any equipment problems to be addressed

To Surgeon, Anaesthetist and Nurse:
☐ What are the key concerns for recovery and management of this patient?

Revised 1 / 2009

This checklist is not intended to be comprehensive. Additions and modifications to fit local practice are encouraged.

Figure 5.2 WHO surgical safety checklist. (Source: WHO Surgical Safety Checklist, http://whqlibdoc.who.int/publications/2009/9789241598590_eng_Checklist.pdf © 2009 World Health Organization. All rights reserved. Used with permission.)

Key Point

Studies have shown that the use of checklists has helped to

- Reduce morbidity and mortality
- Improve communication and the likelihood that staff will speak up about problems they see
- Foster a safety culture
- Drive cost savings

How-to Steps

The "checklist for checklists" shown in Figure 5.3 can help guide the creation of effective checklists. It captures key questions to help you use best practices when developing, drafting, and validating checklists.

5.5.2 Using Checklists Effectively

Key Point

Manual checklists are most effectively used face to face by a team of two or more people in a disciplined way. Checklists can also be computerized, with forcing functions that require tasks to be completed or information to be entered properly before advancing to the next step. In either case, they function as a series of prompts that remind people to do things.

The point of a checklist is not just to check things off or to use as an audit tool after a process has been completed. The idea is to put a process on "pause" at a designated point, review the checklist prompts as a team, and confirm that the necessary quality conditions are in place so that a process may proceed safely and correctly. These "time-outs" for checklist review require all involved to stop and pay full attention, *without interruptions*. If quality conditions have not been met—that is, if something is missing, wrong, or in doubt—the team must be able to *stop the process* until the situation has been addressed.

Of course, we cannot stop to use checklists for every process or operation. But, in situations in which patient harm may occur, in processes that are new or infrequently used, and in processes that are critical to healthcare operations, properly used checklists are an excellent method poka-yoke.

A CHECKLIST FOR CHECKLIST

Development

Does the Checklist:

☐ Do you have clear, concise objectives for your checklist?

Is each item:

☐ A critical safety step and in great danger of being missed?

☐ Not adequately checked by other mechanisms?

☐ Actionable, with a specific response required for each item?

☐ Designed to be read aloud as a verbal check?

☐ One that can be affected by the use of a checklist?

Have you considered:

☐ Adding items that will improve communication among team members?

☐ Involving all members of the team in the checklist creation process?

Drafting

Does the Checklist:

☐ Utilize natural breaks in workflow (pause points)?

☐ Use simple sentence structure and basic language?

☐ Have a title that reflects its objectives?

☐ Have a simple, uncluttered, and logical format?

☐ Fit on one page?

☐ Minimize the use of color?

Is the Font:

☐ Sans serif?

☐ Upper and lower case text?

☐ Large enough to be read easily?

☐ Dark on a light background?

☐ Are there fewer than 10 items per pause point?

☐ Is the date of creation (or revision) clearly marked?

Validation

Have you:

☐ Trialed the checklist with front line users (either in a real or simulated situation)?

☐ Modified the checklist in response to repeated trials?

Does the checklist:

☐ Fit the flow of work?

☐ Detect errors at a time when they can still be corrected?

☐ Can the checklist be completed in a reasonably brief period of time?

☐ Have you made plans for future review and revision of the checklist?

Last updated 1 / 14 / 10

Please note: A checklist is NOT a teaching tool or an algorithm

FIGURE 5.3 A "checklist for checklists" helps ensure effectiveness. (From: *The Checklist Manifesto: How to Get Things Right* by Atul Gawande. Copyright © 2009, 2010 by Atul Gawande. Used by permission of Henry Holt and Company, LLC and Ariadne Labs, a joint center of Brigham and Women's Hospital and Harvard School of Public Health. All rights reserved.)

5.5.3 Stop the Line—Stop the Process

"Stop the line," or "stop the process," means the ability of any worker to stop production or services when a safety or quality problem is identified. Toyota introduced the practice of allowing, and in fact requiring, any worker having a problem to notify a team leader or manager right away. By pulling an *andon cord* or signaling cord, workers could signal a team leader to come to their assistance right away. If the problem could not be solved in a timely manner, the assembly line would stop.

Stopping the process when potential errors or defects are detected is a critical element of jidoka and mistake proofing. In healthcare, we need to build a culture of stopping to fix problems and an attitude of "let's fix it right now" instead of "let's deal with it later" or "let's let someone else deal with it later." Standards and guidelines for stopping the process must be in place and communicated, and everyone must work to root out negative judgments about people who stop the line or question the process.

5.6 PHYSICAL POKA-YOKE

Physical poka-yoke systems are devices built into equipment or facilities to prevent or detect errors or defects. They go back to Sakichi Toyoda's use of autonomation or jidoka as applied to the automatic loom. Toyoda invented a system to stop a loom automatically when a thread broke. In this way, the *error* (a broken thread) could be detected and the machine shut down automatically before it could make a *defect* (flawed textiles). His invention embedded the "human" ability to watch over the loom into the loom itself, freeing workers from this mindless task and permitting them to do more value-added work instead by managing multiple looms at one time.

There are many different types of physical poka-yoke, but the way they are designed generally falls into one of three main categories. Shingo referred to these three approaches as *contact, fixed-value,* and *motion-step* methods, but you can also think of them as *identification, number,* and *sequence* techniques.

5.6.1 Contact or Identification Techniques

Definition

Contact or *identification techniques* work by identifying whether the shape, dimensions, or other physical attributes of a patient, process input, or piece of equipment are correct or correctly positioned. Contact poka-yoke can include sensing devices that detect proper physical contact or alignment with an object. They can also use energy-sensing devices like photoelectric beams as well as electronic sensors such as bar codes or radio-frequency identification tags with scanners. These do not physically touch a product or person but sense when something is not in the expected or correct position or carry identifying information about a patient or supply.

Key Point

Identification approaches do not have to be high tech. *Some of the best contact methods are "passive devices,"* such as guides or blocks that prevent a patient, piece of equipment, or product from being positioned or used incorrectly.

Key Point

Example

Contact methods often involve designing things with an uneven or asymmetrical shape, such as a connector with a pin or a hole on only one end. The connectors used to administer nitrogen and oxygen gases during anesthesia are good examples of the physical contact method. These connectors are designed with a unique combination of pins and holes that make it impossible for the wrong gas cylinder to be connected and wrong gas supplied to a patient (see Figure 5.4).

Small design changes can often make it much easier to catch errors. Problems you notice during your own work can help designers improve processes, products, equipment, and facilities for mistake proofing in the future.

5.6.2 Fixed-Value or Number Techniques

Definition

Fixed-value or *number techniques* work by checking for the correct value or number of something, for example, when

- a fixed number of parts must be attached to something or used during a process,

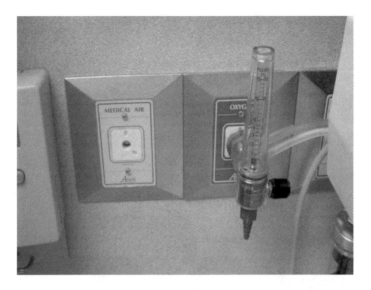

Figure 5.4 Medical gas outlets designed so that the proper valves will fit only in their corresponding outlets use a type of contact or identification poka-yoke technique. (From: http://mmpp.wikispaces. com/file/detail/photo5-10.jpg., accessed August 19, 2014.)

■ a fixed number of repeated operations needs to be performed, or

■ a measurable critical condition has been reached (such as temperature or pressure).

In fixed-value poka-yoke, a device counts the number of parts or times something is done or tracks when a fixed condition is reached. It can then signal completion of the task or process (or warn about the lack of completion). It can also warn when a fixed limit has been exceeded or even shut down a process or operation.

Example

For example, if the water released from a faucet is too hot for safety, a special valve can shut off the water supply (see Figure 5.5). If the temperature of a refrigerator in which vaccines are stored becomes too cold or too warm, a sensor can set off a local or central alarm. And, a temperature-sensing Foley catheter can monitor a patient's core body temperature and signal if it falls outside an upper or lower limit.

The fixed-value approach may use switches such as limit switches that are tripped with each movement, sending a

Figure 5.5 A shutdown valve that stops the water flow from a faucet if it exceeds a fixed temperature is an example of a fixed-value or number poka-yoke. (From: http://mmpp.wikispaces.com/file/detail/photo5-5.jpg, accessed August 19, 2014)

signal to a counter that detects when the right number of movements has happened. Another technique is to measure or count the number of parts in advance; if parts are left over or unaccounted for, workers will know that something is wrong. This technique can be used to prevent surgical sponges from being inadvertently left in a patient during surgery.

5.6.3 Motion-Step or Sequence Techniques

Definition

In the third approach to setting up a poka-yoke, the *motion-step* or *sequence* technique, a device is used to sense whether a motion or step in the process has been carried out within a certain expected time. It can also be used to ensure that things happen in a certain sequence.

The motion-step method may use sensors and devices like a photoelectric switch connected to a timer. If a movement does not happen when it should, the switch signals to stop the equipment or process or gives a warning.

Example

For example, a sensor on the door to a restricted area can allow a limited time in which the door must be opened after swiping an access card. If the proper sequence does not take place (that is, if the door is not opened immediately after the card swipe), the door locks itself (see Figure 5.6).

FIGURE 5.6 Electronic key card locks are a type of motion step or sequence poka-yoke because the door must be opened within a certain time after the key is swiped. (From: © iStockphoto.com/PhotoTalk.)

TAKE FIVE

Take a few minutes to think about these questions and to write down your answers:

- In what kinds of situations in your workplace might you use method poka-yoke such as checklists?
- Can you see any opportunities in your processes to use contact or identification poka-yoke devices? Fixed-value or number poka-yoke? Motion-step or sequence poka-yoke?

5.7 POKA-YOKE SENSORS

Key Point

Physical poka-yoke systems can use sensors; for example, a weight-sensing pad on the bed of a patient at high risk for falls can trigger an alert when contact with the bed is interrupted. Sensors are usually divided into three broad categories:

- Sensors that detect physical contact
- Sensors that detect energy
- Sensors that detect changes in physical conditions

Physical contact-sensing devices work by physically touching something. In many cases, particularly in automated processes, physical contact-sensing devices send an electrical signal when they are touched or released. The signal can stop or start a machine or give a warning that an error has happened.

Energy-sensing devices use energy rather than physical contact to determine whether an error is occurring. For example, a *photoelectric switch* uses beams of light to verify a variety of conditions, such as the proper size or color of an item or the proper supply or movement of equipment or other objects. For example, a pulse oximeter uses a beam of light to monitor the oxygen saturation of blood and triggers an alarm if it drops below a certain level.

Example

Other energy-sensing devices include a *proximity switch,* which can respond to changes in distance from objects and to changes in magnetic force. And, *area sensors* detect random breaks in a fixed area, such as hands placed in hazardous zones.

A third type of poka-yoke sensor, *condition change-sensing devices,* detects changes in physical conditions, such as pressure, temperature, or electrical current. Pressure changes can be detected by pressure gauges and pressure-sensitive switches. Temperature changes can be detected through the use of heat-activated devices, such as thermometers, thermostats, thermistors, and the like. These can be used to monitor patient temperatures or the temperatures of equipment or supplies.

5.8 DEVICES THAT LINK TO POKA-YOKE SENSORS

Key Point

In addition to the sensing devices themselves, poka-yoke systems often include devices that link to the sensors. These devices detect abnormalities in the system that might cause an error, or they transmit information about errors.

For example, *counters* are used to keep track of the number of motions or operations, as signaled by limit switches or other sensing devices. They can be set to signal a control or warning device if the normal number does not occur.

Timers are used when a motion or operation is expected to happen within a certain time. Like counters, they are usually linked to a sensing device and to a control or warning device. Sometimes, timers and counters are used together as well.

Information-transmitting devices include warning devices that use sound or lights to draw attention to abnormalities.

Key Point

A sound usually calls attention to the problem more quickly than a light does. When a light is used, *the "summoning power" of a flashing light is far greater than that of a steady light.* Some warning systems use both light and sound.

There is an ever-growing array of technologies and devices available for mistake proofing, but remember that technology is not always the best answer. Simple devices and reminders are often excellent countermeasures to prevent errors. As with any

Key Point

improvement idea, *it is critical to test any poka-yoke by using the plan–do–check–act (PDCA) cycle, in the gemba* where the work actually happens,* before making it part of standard work.

TAKE FIVE

Take a few minutes to think about these questions and to write down your answers:

- Can you think of situations in your workplace in which energy-sensing devices and sensors that detect changes in physical conditions might be useful? How?
- What about devices that link to poka-yoke sensors? Which of these might be helpful in your work and why?

5.9 SUMMARY

Poka-yoke systems embed a kind of memory into processes, an automatic way of remembering the right, defect-free way to do something. Poka-yoke systems help prevent errors by carrying out two key elements of mistake proofing: 100 percent inspection and quick feedback for corrective action.

---

* The term "gemba" refers to the place where the actual work is performed—e.g., the clinic, the lab, the emergency room, or the billing office.

Poka-yoke systems are most effective when applied in source inspections to catch errors before they occur or before they become defects. Poka-yoke systems can also be used with self-checks and successive checks (informative inspections). This will not eliminate all defects, but it can keep defects from being passed down the line.

Poka-yoke systems regulate processes by using either a control system, which can automatically stop a process, operation, or piece of equipment; or by using a warning system, which signals someone to address the problem. A control system is more certain as a zero-defects method.

There are two main classes of poka-yoke systems used in healthcare: method and physical. Method poka-yoke systems are typically checklist driven and are warning systems. Physical poka-yoke can use contact or identification techniques, fixed-value or number techniques, and motion-step or sequence techniques. Each of these techniques can be used with either control systems or warning systems.

Checklists, whether manual or computer based, provide a series of prompts used at appropriate points of critical processes to prevent errors. They can also represent the steps of an entire process. They are most effective when used by teams during time-outs, coupled with the ability to stop the process if something is wrong. Stopping the process when potential errors or defects are detected is a critical element of jidoka and mistake proofing.

Contact or identification techniques work by detecting whether the shape, dimensions, or other physical attributes of a patient, process input, or piece of equipment are correct or correctly positioned. Contact techniques often take advantage of asymmetrical shapes that make it impossible to position something incorrectly. They can also use sensors such as photoelectric beams or bar codes and scanners.

Fixed-value or number techniques work by checking for the correct value or number of something. They can also shut down a process or trigger an alert when a measurable critical condition has been reached. Motion-step or sequence techniques sense whether a predetermined motion or step in the process has been carried out within a certain expected time or in a certain sequence.

The sensing devices used in poka-yoke systems can include physical contact-sensing devices, energy-sensing devices, and devices that sense changes in physical conditions.

In addition to the sensing devices themselves, poka-yoke systems often include devices that link to the sensors. These devices detect abnormalities in the system that might cause an error, or they transmit information about errors. Sound usually calls attention to the problem more quickly than a light does. When a light is used, the "summoning power" of a flashing light is far greater than that of a steady light.

Many technologies and devices are available for mistake proofing, but technology is not always the best answer. Simple devices and reminders are often excellent countermeasures to prevent errors. Any poka-yoke should be tested in the gemba before making it part of standard work.

5.10 REFLECTIONS

Now that you have completed this chapter, take 5 minutes to think about these questions and to write down your answers:

- What did you learn from reading this chapter that stands out as particularly useful or interesting?
- Do you have any questions about the topics presented in this chapter? If so, what are they?
- What information do you still need to fully understand the ideas presented in this chapter?
- How can you obtain this information?

Chapter 6

Examples of Poka-Yoke Applications

6.1 LEARNING FROM EXAMPLES OF POKA-YOKE APPLICATIONS

Key Point

This chapter presents examples of poka-yoke systems being used in healthcare. *It also provides a variety of applications to help you understand how poka-yoke systems are used.* These examples may also give you some ideas about how to apply poke-yoke systems in your own workplace.

As you study the examples, notice that a poka-yoke system need not be elaborate and expensive. In fact, many solutions are simple and inexpensive. Many poka-yoke applications were suggested by clinicians and hospital staff—the people who know patients, healthcare processes, and equipment the best. As you read the chapter, think about how a poka-yoke system might help your own processes become error free.

Key Point

And remember, these are just examples. *All poka-yoke applications should be tested on the gemba, in your own setting, before being adopted as standard work.*

6.2 METHOD POKA-YOKE EXAMPLES

6.2.1 Thoracic Surgery Checklist

Figure 6.1 shows an example of an adult cardiac surgery checklist template developed by the Society of Thoracic Surgeons (STS). It is an adaptation from the World Health Organization (WHO) Surgical Safety Checklist (see Figure 5.2 in Chapter 5). Checklists should be customized and tested to ensure that they are suitable for specific settings. See the Appendix for details on sources of downloadable checklist templates and examples.

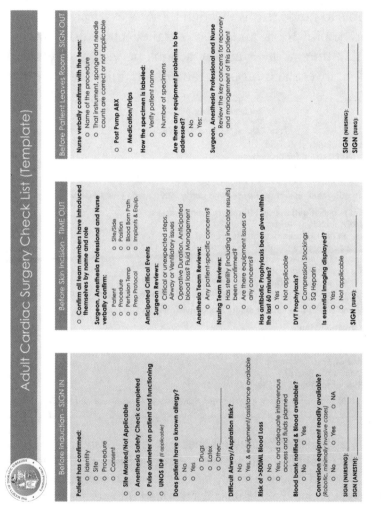

Figure 6.1 Template for an adult cardiac surgery checklist. (© The Society of Thoracic Surgeons. Used with permission. All rights reserved.)

6.2.2 Red Event Safety Alert, Incident Command Checklist

Figure 6.2 shows a checklist used to facilitate immediate assessment on the gemba of a serious safety event. This is an example of a top-level checklist used to help mistake proof a less-frequently used process. The checklist is set up as a series of prompts to guide teams through the process, to direct them to other helpful tools and more detailed checklists, and to ensure that they address all key actions necessary to contain a situation, investigate properly, and communicate effectively.

Red Event Safety Alert
Incident Command Checklist
For AOC or Nursing Supervisor

☐ **Assure situation is stabilized**
    ☐ Patient is cared for properly
        ☐ Other patient needs are being met
        ☐ Staff involved is present and cared for

☐ **Identify other team members needed and notify PBX to page (See Decision Matrix Tool)**

☐ **Coordinate Investigation using Response Team Checklist**
    ☐ Is RCA toolkit present?
    ☐ Are all the right team members present?
        ☐ Is all evidence documented and secured?
    ☐ Has the family been notified?
    ☐ Has media relations been notified?
    ☐ Is there a need for chaplain services?
    ☐ Have countermeasures been immediately put in place to prevent further harm?

☐ **Initiate and coordinate Patient Safety Event Investigation Summary**

☐ **Notify the following:**
    ☐ CEO
    ☐ Executive Team
    ☐ Medical Staff leadership
    ☐ Chair of the Board
    ☐ Chair of the Board Quality Committee

☐ **Hand off Patient Safety Event Investigation Summary to appropriate VP for RCA**

FIGURE 6.2 Incident command checklist for following proper procedures after a serious safety event. (From UCSF Benioff Children's Hospital Oakland. This is a facility-specific form and was not designed or intended to have global applicability. Used with permission.)

6.2.3 Chart Preparation Checklist

Figures 6.3 (A) Before and (B) After (next page) show a chemotherapy medication reconciliation checklist used to support standard work in chart preparation and handoffs. The team devised this checklist and communication tool to track required studies, labs, and medication changes between visits for enrolled patients. It also alerts team members if a custom medication list is currently being provided by one of the case managers, saving people rework and phone calls for clarification. The checklist is started at the end of a clinic visit and built in to the flow of information between visits. As shown in the before and after pictures, this checklist moves the team past the need for individual "creative" workflows, workarounds, and thousands of sticky notes and highlighters and helps mistake proof their work so that it is right the first time.

Before

FIGURE 6.3 (A) Chart preparation for chemotherapy, before improvement. (From UCSF Benioff Children's Hospital Oakland. Used with permission.)

After

FIGURE 6.3 (B) Chart preparation checklist for chemotherapy medication reconciliation. (From UCSF Benioff Children's Hospital Oakland, 2013. This is a facility-specific form and was not designed or intended to have global applicability. Used with permission.)

6.2.4 Rounding Checklist

Figure 6.4 shows another example of a checklist that supports standard work, this time in the frequently used process of hospital rounds. The original checklist was formatted into a visual aid, with prompts designed to prevent teams from making mistakes by missing items during rounds. The prompts follow the most effective sequence for the process, with color coding to call out the roles and responsibilities of each member of the rounding team. Standard times are listed for each part of the process.

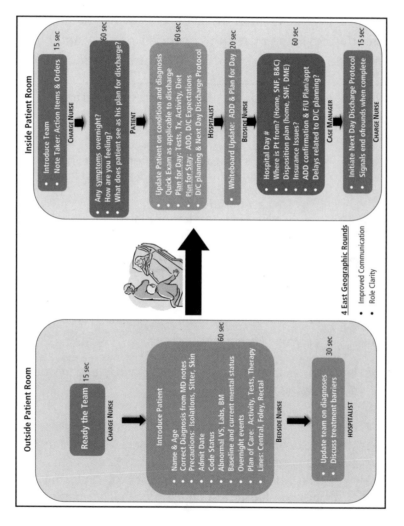

FIGURE 6.4 Rounding checklist formatted as a visual aid. (From Sutter Health East Bay Region, Alta Bates. Used with permission.)

6.2.5 Clinician Previsit Checklist

Figure 6.5 shows an even simpler rendering of a checklist formatted as a visual aid designed to help prevent mistakes in a clinic. The acronym REACH (review, edit, add, check, huddle) outlines the key steps in the previsit process and serves as a mnemonic device, with the visual aid serving as a reminder of what each step involves. Following the checklist consistently prevents errors in the previsit process and eliminates rework, delays, and wasted time during patient visits.

Clinician Pre-Visit Check list "REACH for the sky, Partner!"
- o **R**eview Pending orders folder
- o **E**dit orders as needed
- o **A**dd orders/tests as needed
- o **C**heck schedule for potential No Shows
- o **H**uddle with MA 2 days prior to check:
  - o Appropriate work load?
  - o Last minute Pt review
  - o Needed supplies or plans

FIGURE 6.5 A visual aid for the previsit procedure at a clinic. (Based on a checklist used at Sutter Health East Bay Medical Foundation. Used with permission.)

TAKE FIVE

Take a few minutes to think about these questions and to write down your answers:

- Can you think of situations in your workplace where method poka-yoke and visual aids could be useful in preventing mistakes?
- How would you describe the causes of problems that might have led to the creation of these types of mistake-proofing examples? Can you think of other ways to solve them?

6.2.6 Electronic Health Systems

Electronic health record systems can provide a kind of automated checklist function for many types of processes. In the example shown in Figure 6.6, one such system has detected a potentially dangerous drug interaction for a medication ordered for a patient. Although the warning can be overridden, the system provides a high level of mistake proofing. For a high-risk alert, it interrupts and requires the physician to make a decision before continuing.

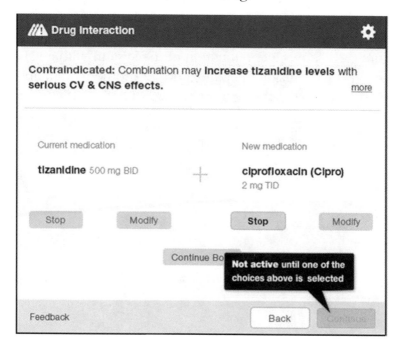

Figure 6.6 Electronic health system automated check, or alert, function for drug interactions. (From Belden, et al. *Inspired EHRs: Designing for Clinicians*, Figure 6.4, http://inspiredehrs.org/designing-for-clinicians/drug-alerts.php. © 2014 The Curators of the University of Missouri. All rights reserved. Reprinted under the Apache 2.0 open source license, http://opensource.org/licenses/Apache-2.0)

6.3 CONTACT OR IDENTIFICATION POKA-YOKE EXAMPLES

6.3.1 Integrated Color-Coding Systems

Color coding does not preclude mistakes, but when an integrated system uses multiple, consistent color cues combined with text, it can provide an excellent warning poka-yoke. At one facility, yellow is the color used to identify a patient with a high risk for falls. As shown in Figure 6.7A, the integrated system includes a yellow wristband and patient information card that combine color and text and yellow slip-proof socks. Figure 6.7B shows a continuation of the system with a yellow square posted outside the patient door. Another cue might be a yellow blanket at the bottom of the patient's bed.

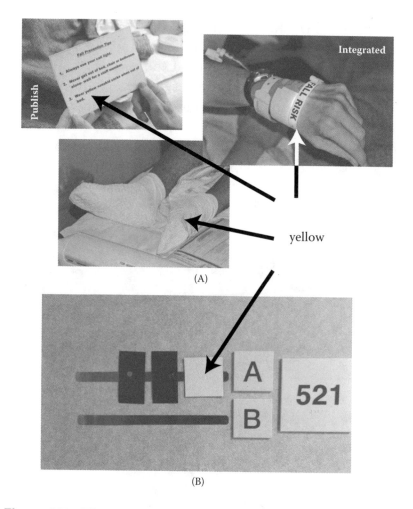

yellow

Figure 6.7 (A) and (B) Integrated color-coding systems for identifying high-risk patients. (From California Pacific Medical Center. Used with permission.)

6.3.2 Other Color-Coding Poka-Yoke Examples

Color coding can be used in many ways to help mistake proof processes. Although it is not a *control* mechanism, it can provide effective *warnings*. For example, high-risk medication bags and lines can be color coded to help prevent confusion (see Figure 6.8A). The "after" image on this poster shows that the intravenous lines have been tagged and color coded to correspond to their medication bags and pumps.

Interruptions are a frequent cause of errors and mistakes in healthcare. The nurse in Figure 6.8B is wearing a bright orange "no interruptions" belt. It alerts others that she is administering medications or performing other sensitive work and should not be interrupted.

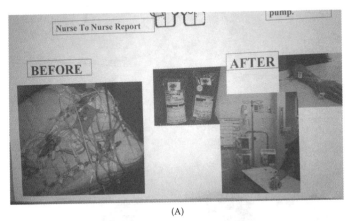

(A)

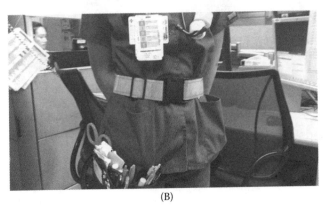

(B)

Figure 6.8 (A) and (B) Color coding used to warn about high-risk medications and to prevent staff interruptions. (From California Pacific Medical Center. Used with permission)

6.3.3 Wristbands with Bar Codes or Radio-Frequency Identification Tags

Patient wristbands are commonly used as poka-yoke devices. They can provide a way to positively identify patients by printing the patient's name and other information and by using "automatic" identification techniques such as bar codes that can be scanned, as shown in Figure 6.9. Wristbands with radio-frequency identification (RFID) tags can also carry information about patient identification and provide links to medical records. These automated identification techniques are also used to assist with medication management and with maintaining electronic health records for patients.

Color coding on the wristband, or the use of additional wristbands, provides alerts to staff of special patient needs, including latex allergy, medication or other allergies, fall risks, do not resuscitate (DNR) orders, and even restricted extremities where intravenous lines or blood pressure cuffs should not be placed. Efforts to standardize color-coded alerts are ongoing.

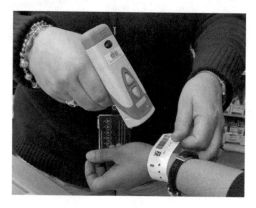

Figure 6.9 Patient wristband with bar code and scanner. (From *Clinical Center News*, National Institutes of Health, June 2014.)

6.3.4 Tactile Signals on Wrong Buttons

Figure 6.10 shows a simple way to used tactile signals as a warning poka-yoke, in this case to identify buttons that should not be pressed on a machine used to compound solutions for continuous renal replacement therapy. Self-stick Velcro pieces were applied to buttons that should never be touched after the initial setup. Visual reminders (sticky notes on the machine) had not been enough to prevent technicians from accidentally changing to the wrong settings. These tactile signals were able to prevent another incident.

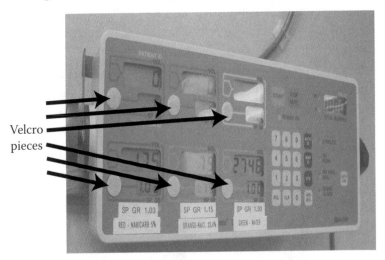

Figure 6.10 Contact poka-yoke can use tactile signals, shown here to identify proper usage of equipment. (From http://mmpp.wiki-spaces.com/bad+buttons, Therese Staublin, PharmD, St. Francis Hospital and Health Centers, accessed August 19, 2014.)

6.3.5 Throat Pack Identification

The "contact" poka-yoke shown in Figure 6.11 identifies patients who have a throat pack inserted during surgery. Used to absorb matter and prevent it from entering the esophagus or lungs, a throat pack can obstruct the patient's airway if it is retained after surgery. This simple poka-yoke is now standard work at one hospital to help mistake proof the removal of throat packs following surgery.

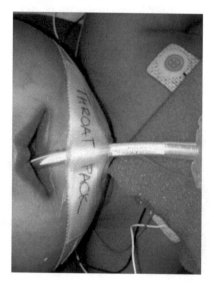

Figure 6.11 A contact poka-yoke used to identify throat packs helps ensure removal after surgery. (From UCSF Benioff Children's Hospital Oakland. This is a facility-specific application and was not designed or intended to have global applicability. Used with permission.)

6.3.7 Shrink-Wrapping on Dangerous Medications

Figure 6.12 shows an example that combines visual and tactile cues in a contact or identification poka-yoke. Medications that can cause paralysis are shrink-wrapped with a bright red cover. This poka-yoke visually alerts the person administering the medication that it is dangerous. It also requires the person to physically remove the label, a tactile signal that takes time to perform and is even more difficult to overlook.

Other ways to prevent medication confusion include bar coding as well as using labels to clearly distinguish the names of look-alike or sound-alike drugs (e.g., cefTAZidime, cloNAZepam).

Figure 6.12 Shrink-wrapping high-risk medications combines visual and tactile signals in a contact poka-yoke. (From http://mmpp. wikispaces.com/ShrinkWrap, accessed August 19, 2014.)

TAKE FIVE

Take a few minutes to think about these questions and to write down your answers:

- Can you think of situations in your workplace where contact, or identification, poka-yoke devices could be useful in preventing mistakes?
- How would you describe the causes of problems that might have led to the creation of these types of mistake-proofing examples? Can you think of other ways to solve them?

6.4 FIXED-VALUE OR NUMBER POKA-YOKE EXAMPLES

6.4.1 Surgical Sponge-Counting Systems

Fixed-value, or number, poka-yoke can help prevent mistakes by automatically detecting the right *number* of something. For example, surgical sponges can be accounted for using sponge counter bags like the one shown in Figure 6.13. Retained surgical items can cause serious patient harm and even death as well as significant cost. Counter bags for sponges, the most frequently retained items, have a compartment for each sponge so a nurse can easily see if a sponge is missing. In a sense, the bags "automatically" count the sponges. Approaches that are more technological include the use of sponges embedded with radio-frequency tags or labeled with bar codes that can be tracked using a detector or scanner.

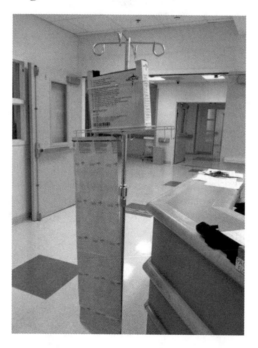

Figure 6.13 Counting systems for surgical sponges are a fixed-value or number approach to prevent retained surgical items.

6.4.2 Automatically Timed Processes

Another type of number or fixed value that can be mistake proofed is *time*. A simple example of a poka-yoke device that helps ensure a process takes place for the right length of time is an electric toothbrush with a timer, shown in Figure 6.14. The toothbrush signals when a person has brushed for the recommended amount of time, preventing the mistake of ineffective "underbrushing." Some toothbrushes also have quadrant timers that signal when it is time to move to brushing another mouth quadrant.

Figure 6.14 Fixed-value approaches can help ensure that a process runs for the right amount of time, for example, automatically timed toothbrushes. (From http://commons.wikimedia.org/wiki/File:Electrical_toothbrush_20050717_001.jpg.)

6.4.3 Automated External Defibrillator

Fixed-value poka-yoke techniques can also monitor whether a fixed *condition* has been reached for a process to proceed. For example, as shown in Figures 6.15A and 6.15B, an automated external defibrillator contains technology that automatically detects a patient's heart rhythm and administers a shock only if the patient is in ventricular fibrillation or tachycardia.

(A)

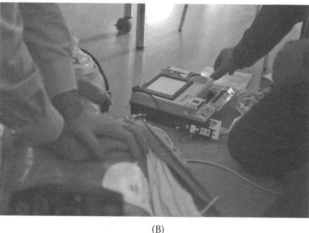

(B)

Figure 6.15 (A) and (B) Automated external defibrillators monitor for the right condition, another form of fixed-value mistake proofing. (Figure 6.15A from http://commons.wikimedia.org/wiki/File:AED_open_cutout.jpg, by Owain Davies. Figure 6.15B from http://commons.wikimedia.org/wiki/File:AED_open_cutout.jpg, by Rama.)

6.4.4 Bed Angle Visual Aid

Keeping the head of a patient's bed elevated at the proper angle can be a critical protocol for preventing ventilator-acquired pneumonia and other conditions. But, bed angle indicators can be difficult to read, especially from a distance. A simple solution developed by one team was to apply a prominent sign on beds that should be raised, as shown in Figure 6.16. This simple device serves as a visual control that helps alert staff to maintain the proper position on beds of critically ill patients. Although it does not guarantee that the bed will be raised to the correct position, the team found that staff quickly grew accustomed to observing whether the sign was at the correct angle.

Figure 6.16 This bed angle sign shows how visual aids can help mistake proof for the right fixed value or number. (From http://mmpp. wikispaces.com/hob30, accessed August 19, 2014.)

6.4.5 Pulse Oximeter

Fixed-value or number poka-yoke can also detect whether a number falls within a normal *range*. For example, a pulse oximeter, as shown in Figure 6.17, monitors a patient's oxygen saturation level using a photodetector to analyze blood oxygen levels. If the level falls below a certain value, an alarm will sound.

Figure 6.17 A pulse oximeter automatically checks whether a number falls within an acceptable range. (From http://commons. wikimedia.org/wiki/File:Wrist-oximeter.jpg.)

TAKE FIVE

Take a few minutes to think about these questions and to write down your answers:

- Can you think of situations in your workplace where fixed-value or number poka-yoke devices could be useful in preventing mistakes?
- How would you describe the causes of problems that might have led to the creation of these types of mistake-proofing examples? Can you think of other ways to solve them?

6.5 MOTION-STEP OR SEQUENCE POKA-YOKE EXAMPLES

6.5.1 Oral Care Pegboard

Figure 6.18 shows an oral care pegboard designed by an intensive care unit (ICU) nurse. Hung in ICU rooms, this simple board helps to mistake proof the provision of oral care in the right sequence at specific intervals throughout the day. The board provides a visual cue but is also stocked at the beginning of the day with the needed implements and supplies in the correct order, each hung on the appropriate time peg.

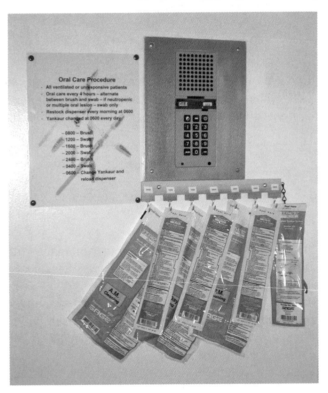

Figure 6.18 An oral care pegboard is a warning-type sequence poka-yoke. (From http://mmpp.wikispaces.com/file/detail/Oral_Care_Board.JPG, accessed November 10, 2014.)

6.5.2 Glucose Test Reminder

To help remind patients to test their insulin level before eating, one hospital created a simple visual alert, as shown in Figure 6.19. This simple visual management technique helps ensure that diabetic patients follow the proper sequence of activities before meals.

Figure 6.19 This glucose test visual aid reminds patients to follow the right sequence. (From California Pacific Medical Center. Used with permission.)

6.5.3 Hand Hygiene Monitoring Systems

Some facilities are moving beyond visual controls such as posters and signs that remind staff to wash hands and are installing higher-level mistake-proofing systems. These include everything from direct observation of hand hygiene practices by trained observers to automated systems that can detect whether a clinician has washed hands before and after certain tasks.

World Health Organization guidelines have led to a list of "five moments for hand hygiene":*

1. Before patient contact.
2. Before aseptic task.
3. After body fluid exposure risk.
4. After patient contact
5. After contact with patient surroundings

A variety of automated systems can now help detect whether hand hygiene is being performed in the right sequence before and after some of these tasks.

One system uses badges worn by healthcare workers. A worker's badge turns green when hand hygiene has been performed. Monitors near a patient bed "see" whether the badge is green. If not, the badge vibrates to warn the worker.

Another system uses wireless devices that detect when point-of-care sanitizer dispensers are used. The data is captured and used to generate reports that provide feedback to help teams improve. Would you consider this a true poka-yoke or a helpful type of informative inspection?

---

* See http://www.who.int/gpsc/tools/Five_moments/en/.

6.5.4 Sheathed Needles

Figure 6.20 shows an example of a needle designed with an attached protective sheath used to prevent accidental needle sticks. As the phlebotomist withdraws the needle after a blood draw, he or she pushes forward the cover portion (attached just above the needle) with his or her thumb to prevent any further sticks. This poka-yoke can be thought of as a motion-step or sequence technique because it helps ensure that the needle is covered and the technician is protected right after blood is drawn.

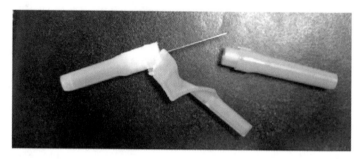

Figure 6.20   A sheathed needle helps to prevent needle sticks by ensuring that the needle is covered as it is withdrawn, another type of sequence poka-yoke.

TAKE FIVE

Take a few minutes to think about these questions and to write down your answers:

- Can you think of situations in your workplace where motion-step poka-yoke devices could be useful in preventing mistakes?
- How would you describe the causes of problems that might have led to the creation of these types of mistake-proofing examples? Can you think of other ways to solve them?

6.6 SUMMARY

Examples of poka-yoke systems as they are used in health-care were presented in this chapter. They are designed to help you understand how poka-yoke systems are put to use and may also give you ideas about how to apply poka-yoke systems in your own workplace.

Poka-yoke systems need not be fancy or expensive. Many of the solutions presented in this chapter are actually simple and inexpensive. Also, many of the solutions were suggested by clinicians and hospital staff—the people who know the equipment and processes the best. How can poka-yoke systems help your own process become error free?

6.7 REFLECTIONS

Now that you have completed this chapter, take 5 minutes to think about these questions and to write down your answers:

- What did you learn from reading this chapter that stands out as particularly useful or interesting?
- Do you have any questions about the topics presented in this chapter? If so, what are they?
- What information do you still need to fully understand the ideas presented in this chapter?
- How can you obtain this information?

Chapter 7

Reflections and Conclusions

7.1 REFLECTING ON WHAT YOU HAVE LEARNED

Key Point

An important part of learning is reflecting on what you have learned. Without this step, learning cannot take place effectively because few connections can be made to your existing knowledge and thus little useful information can be fixed in long-term memory. Now that you have come to the end of this book, we would like to ask you to reflect on what you have learned. We suggest you take 10 minutes to write down answers to the following questions:

- What did you learn from reading this book that stands out as particularly useful or interesting?
- Do you have any questions about Zero Quality Control (ZQC) or mistake proofing? If so, what are they?
- What ideas, tools, and techniques have you learned that will be most useful in your own work? How will they be useful?
- What ideas, tools, and techniques have you learned that will be least useful in your work? Why would they not be useful?

7.2 APPLYING WHAT YOU HAVE LEARNED

7.2.1 Possibilities for Applying What You Have Learned

The way you apply what you have learned will, of course, depend on your situation. If your organization is launching a full-scale mistake-proofing effort as part of a lean (or Six Sigma or Lean Sigma) transformation, you should have ample opportunity to apply what you have learned from this book in your own workplace. In this case, you may be included in a team of people who are responsible for improving a certain work area. You may have time for improvement structured into your workday and may be responsible for reporting the results of your activities on a regular basis.

At the other end of the spectrum, your organization may have no immediate plans to mistake-proof processes. In this case, the extent to which you can apply what you have learned will depend on how much control you have over your own schedule, work flow, and work area.

7.2.2 Your Personal Action Plan

Key Point You may or may not be in a management position that permits you to plan or implement mistake proofing of processes on a grand scale. Whatever your situation, *we suggest you create a personal action plan for how you will begin applying the information you have learned from this book.* You might start by referring to your own notes about the techniques and tools you think will be most useful to you, then writing down ideas in response to the following questions:

- What mistake-proofing techniques can I implement right now that will make my job easier, better, or more efficient?
- How can I involve my coworkers in the implementation of what I have learned?

When you have answered these questions, we suggest that you commit to completing the things you have written down in a specific period of time and to making a new plan at the end of that time period. In each phase, you need to be asking and answering the following questions:

- How can we create inspection in every step of our processes?
- How can we ensure errors are always corrected as soon as possible and as close to the point of origin as possible?
- How can we create the standard work and tools to guarantee error-proof processes?
- How can we make sure everyone feels empowered to stop the line for safety?

Key Point

When implementing anything, it is often good to start with something small that you can comfortably finish in the time you have allowed yourself. If the project is too ambitious or time consuming, you can easily become discouraged and give up.

Also, projects you can work on for short periods of time whenever you get a chance are ideal in the beginning. For example, you might decide to use mistake-proofing techniques in a medication room to reduce inadvertent medication errors by improving the way medications are organized and labeled. Alternatively, you might work to mistake proof a registration process to improve the quality and timeliness of information gathered from patients.

7.2.3 Opportunities for Further Learning

Here are some ways to learn more about ZQC and mistake proofing:

- Find other reference material on this subject. Several resources are listed in the Appendix.
- If your organization is already applying mistake-proofing techniques, visit other areas to see how they are doing it.

■ Find out how other healthcare organizations have used mistake proofing.

7.3 CONCLUSION

Mistake proofing is more than a series of techniques. It is a fundamental approach to the error-free production of healthcare services to the benefit of both patients and staff. We hope this book has given you a taste of how and why this method can be helpful and effective for you in your work. We welcome your stories about how you apply mistake proofing in your own workplace.

Appendix

FURTHER READING ABOUT MISTAKE PROOFING AND RELATED TOPICS

Gawande, Atul. *The Checklist Manifesto: How to Get Things Right.* New York: Picador Reprint edition, 2011.

Groopman, Jerome E. *How Doctors Think.* Boston: Houghton Mifflin, 2007.

Grout, John. *Mistake-Proofing the Design of Health Care Processes.* (Prepared under an IPA with Berry College.) AHRQ Publication No. 07-0020. Rockville, MD: Agency for Healthcare Research and Quality, May 2007.

Kahneman, Daniel. *Thinking, Fast and Slow.* New York: Farrar, Straus and Giroux, 2011.

Shingo, Shigeo. *Zero Quality Control: Source Inspection and the Poka-yoke System.* New York: Productivity Press, 1986.

FURTHER READING ABOUT LEAN HEALTHCARE

Rona Consulting Group and Productivity Press, Thomas L. Jackson, editor. Lean Tools for Healthcare Series. New York: Productivity Press. Series titles published to date:

- *5S for Healthcare.* 2009. Imparts the information needed to understand and implement this essential lean methodology for organization in the health-care workplace. Includes helpful how-to-steps and practical examples.
- *Kaizen Workshops for Lean Healthcare.* 2012. Describes what a kaizen improvement event entails and details all the phases necessary to conduct a successful kaizen workshop in healthcare. Covers planning, key roles, implementation, presentation of results, and ongoing follow-up.
- *Mapping Clinical Value Streams.* 2013. Details how to use the powerful value stream mapping process in healthcare to observe and depict clinical processes as they are, and to envision and configure them without waste.

The book defines value, value streams, and service families in clinical settings, then shows how to map the current state, discover opportunities to eliminate wastes and waiting, to create "flow" or "pull," and to map your future state processes.

■ *Standard Work for Lean Healthcare*. 2011. Explains how standard work can be used in healthcare to increase patient safety and reduce costs. The book illustrates how standardization can help establish best practices for performing daily work and why it should be the cornerstone for all continuous improvement efforts. Presented in an easy-to-assimilate format, the book describes work in terms of cycle time, work in process, takt time, and layout.

Rona Consulting Group, *The Lean Healthcare Dictionary: An Illustrated Guide to Using the Language of Lean Management in Healthcare*. New York: Productivity Press, 2015. Defines essential lean and healthcare terms to help create a common language for anyone involved in lean healthcare improvement activities.

Graban, Mark. *Lean Hospitals: Improving Quality, Patient Safety, and Employee Satisfaction*, second edition. New York: Productivity Press, 2011. This book explains why and how lean can be used to improve quality, safety, and morale in healthcare. Graban highlights the benefits of lean methods and explains how lean manufacturing staples such as value stream mapping can help hospital personnel identify and eliminate waste, effectively preventing delays for patients, reducing wasted motion for caregivers, and improving quality of care.

Grunden, Naida. *The Pittsburgh Way to Efficient Healthcare: Improving Patient Care Using Toyota Based Methods*. New York: Productivity Press, 2008. A look at how principles borrowed from industry can be applied to make healthcare safer and, in doing so, make it more efficient and less costly. The book presents a compilation of case studies from units in Pittsburgh-area hospitals that have applied industrial principles successfully, making patients safer and employees more satisfied.

USEFUL WEBSITES

Agency for Healthcare Research and Quality (www.ahrq.gov). The AHRQ website offers many valuable resources, including a section devoted to quality and patient safety.

John Grout's Mistake Proofing Center (http://www.mistakeproofing.com). Shingo Prize-winner John Grout's websites devoted to mistake proofing, a key technique for kaizen and lean operations generally. An entire website within the center is devoted to mistake-proofing applications in healthcare.

Institute for Healthcare Improvement (www.ihi.org). The IHI website provides information and resources on many improvement-related topics and includes a section focused on patient safety.

Lean Blog (http://www.leanblog.org/). A blog founded by author Mark Graban about lean in factories, hospitals, and the world around us.

National Quality Forum (www.qualityforum.org). The NQF works to catalyze improvements in healthcare, with patient safety as one primary area of focus; the NQF website includes tools and reports on measures, as well as information on ongoing projects.

Productivity Press (www.productivitypress.com). The website of Productivity Press, where you may order the Lean Healthcare Series titles, the *Lean Healthcare Dictionary*, and many other seminal and award-winning books about lean, total quality management, and total productive maintenance.

Project Check (www.projectcheck.org). Provides online access to various medical checklists, including a downloadable version of "A Checklist for Checklists."

Rona Consulting Group (http://www.ronaconsulting.com). The official website of series editor Thomas L. Jackson and his partners at Rona Consulting Group.

Society of Thoracic Surgeons, The (http://www.sts.org/quality-research-patient-safety/patient-safety). The Patient Safety section of The Society of Thoracic Surgeons website includes downloadable surgical checklist templates for adult cardiac, general thoracic, and congenital heart surgeries.

World Health Organization (http://www.who.int/entity/patientsafety/en/). Provides many valuable resources, including patient safety and surgical safety checklists with implementation and adaptation guidelines; hand hygiene implementation tools; patient engagement tools; and more.

Index

A

abnormality, 18
absorbing information, 2–4
administrative wastes, 8
adult cardiac surgery, *see* Thoracic surgery
    checklist
alarms, 45
ambiguity, zero, 13
anchoring, 22
andons, 39, 50
anesthesia example, 51
antichaos principle, 14
application, personal, 86, *see also* Examples;
    Poka-yoke applications
area sensors, 55
Argyris, Chris, 14
asymmetrical shape, 51
automated external defibrillator, 77
automatically timed processes, 76
automatic loom, 50
autonomation, *see also* Stop the line/process
  lean healthcare management, 12, 13
  physical poka-yoke, 50
  quality at the source, 29
availability, 22

B

background information, 4, 7–9
badges, hand hygiene, 82
bar-coded wristbands, 71
bar codes, 51
bed angle visual aid, 78
benefits, mistake proofing, 19

blaming, 17
Boeing Aircraft Company, 7
buttons, tactile signals, 72

C

call light, 45
cardiac surgery, *see* Thoracic surgery checklist
Centers for Medicare and Medicaid Services, 9
central line-associated bloodstream
    infection (CLABSI), 46
chart preparation checklist, 63–64
Cheaper by the Dozen, 9
checker, food tray line, 32
checklists, *see also* Method poka-yoke systems
    and techniques
  basic concepts, 43, 46, 48, 57
  chart preparation, 63–64
  checklists for checklists, 48, 49, 91
  clinician previsit, 66
  effective use, 48
  incident command, 62
  method poka-yoke systems, 46–48, 49
  rounding, 64–65
  thoracic surgery, 60–61
CLABSI (central line-associated bloodstream
    infection), 46
clinician previsit checklist, 66
closure, premature, 22
cognitive errors, 21
color-coding systems, 45, 68–70
communication errors, 20–21
condition change-sensing devices, 55
conditions, controlling, 17, 23–25